2014

Happy 50th Birthday
Tim

Love,
Mom

A Sand Hills Revelation

THE
HISTORY - LEGACY - LEGEND
OF
BLANEY - ELGIN
SOUTH CAROLINA

by MADGE BLACK STRICKLAND

Published for the Blaney-Elgin Musuem and Historical Society, Elgin, South Carolina.

Publishing Coordinator: David C Strickland , San Antonio, Texas
Designer: Sonia H.Villarreal, San Antonio, Texas
Printing: Cenveo Clarke Printing, San Antonio, Texas

November 2013 - Printed in the U.S.A.

1 2 3 4 5 6 D C B A
ISBN - 978-1-4675-9151-5

For the Sand Hills Generations
May you flourish forever...

To Jim Gardner
Love at Christmas!
Madge B. Strickland

ACKNOWLEDGMENTS

It is not humanly possible to acknowledge all who have helped in the research and publication of this book, and I apologize to those who might be omitted from this listing. Assistance and support for this project have been expressed in so many ways -- a smile, a hug or a word of encouragement, interviews gladly given, photographs, illustrations, maps, books and documents furnished, stories and valuable information provided, suggestions and even criticism offered. Though overwhelmed at times, I have realized anew that one never gets to first base alone. It is only through a cooperative team effort that we move on to meet our goals. Only six letters say it all........THANKS!

David Strickland - Publishing Coordination/Internet Research
Cathy Strickland - Editing
Judy Darby-Buchanan - Photographer/Town Hall Records
Anna Chason - Photographer
Dusty Rhodes- Photographer
Pete James - Chief Encourager/books/articles
Shirley Miles - History Advisor/videos/articles
Doris Kling - Good Advice & Historical Information
Billie Nelson, Preston Goff, Jean Watson, Sandra & Ed Jones, Jimmy Nelson, John Henry Rabon, Lois Carns, Sivas Ross Branham, Novis Boulware, Gayle Ross, Afon & Van Strickland, Chief Harold Brown, Vivian Gardner, Lem & Nancy Wooten, Nettie Campbell, Jimmie Rose, Carol Adams, Ken Jackson, Ruth Brown, Glenna Brown Kaiser, Vickie Summerton, Myra Monroe, Joe & Mary Tate, Phyllis Martin, Mike Craven, George Marthers, Fred Davidson, Robin & Nelson McLeod, Glenda Marsh, Dan Griffin, Blanche Riley, Jerry Lewis, Tony Casey, Dotty Martin, Bradley Branham, Dallas Phelps, Wilma Campbell, Valerie Hyman, Darlene Strickland, Vera & Wayne Nelson, Claude Campbell, Peggy Wilke, Tracie Sherceh, Eleanor Kelly, Juanita Koon Aldrich, Harry Brooks Cochran, Sally Emanuel, Melanie Portee, Beth Hyman, Loretta Qualls, Jeannie Potter, Patti Potter Coleman, Sandra Smith, Judy Brock, Margie Crowley, and Parker Pruitt.

Contents

Contents

Chapter I

In The Beginning

A treaty signed on July 2, 1755, between Royal Governor James Glen of Charleston (term 1743 - 1756) who represented the King of England, and the Cherokee Indian Nation at Saluda Old Town, accelerated the settlement of middle and upper South Carolina, which included Kershaw County and a future community first called Jeffers, then Blaney, and finally Elgin, South Carolina.

Prior to this, in 1666, an Englishman named Henry Woodward, a surgeon, remained with the Indians at Port Royal Sound in what became South Carolina after his colony-seeking English expedition left for home. He traded with the Port Royal and interior Indians and learned their customs and language so well that the Spanish from St. Augustine, Florida, considered him a threat to their designs on the area. When the English expedition returned to Port Royal Sound in 1670 to continue their search for a site to start a colony, Woodward persuaded them that, because of the ongoing Spanish threats, they should go sixty miles further up the coast to establish a colony.

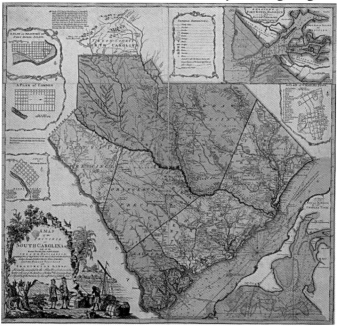

Map of the Province of South Carolina, c.1773 by James Cook

An English settlement along the banks of the Ashley River proved successful in establishing a permanent colony out of the wilderness in South Carolina. Charles Towne (Charleston) was thus established in the Province of South Carolina in 1670. The settlers soon found themselves defending their hard-won land from threats by the Spanish from St. Augustine. They struggled to establish trade and good relations with the native Indians, and securing a reliable source of food was challenging. The colonies in the Carolinas (North & South) were first named "Carolana" (Latin "Carolus") for King Charles II of England. The spelling eventually was changed to "Carolina".

In 1709, another Englishman, John Lawson, a surveyor in Charles Towne, published a journal of his travels in the backcountry of central "Carolina". He surveyed the length of the Wateree River in 1701 and encountered the Wateree and Catawba Indians, describing the natives and their living conditions, and habitats, as well as the area's animals and weather conditions. His journal, published in England, was of great interest and encouragement to those contemplating settling in the new country.

Disputes and dissent over governance of the province led to the division between North and South Carolina which became complete in 1712.

A devastating smallpox outbreak in 1718 among the colonists and Indians alike made creating homesteads and keeping the peace even harder.

In 1719, a rebellion broke out with the colonists complaining that the British proprietors had not protected them enough in the Yamasee War (1715-1717) with the Indians who had ravaged the backcountry of the colony and against the attacks of the neighboring Spanish in Queen Ann's War (1702-1713).

In 1720, the King appointed a royal governor for South Carolina to replace the Proprietary Governors of the past (James Monroe II).

Within the first fifty years of colonization, the English settlement spread into the surrounding countryside, building plantations which were worked by slaves (the slaves outnumbered their masters 2-1). By the 1750s South Carolina was well on its way to becoming a colony to be reckoned with, and the port at Charles Towne was very active in Trans-Atlantic trading.

From a wilderness crossed by Indian trading pathways, like the Great Catawba Trading Path which ran near the Wateree River in the midlands gradually going north and east, to today's U. S. Highway # 1 (which essentially follows the "Cheraw Road" or the "Fall Line Rd., from the north to south, through the sand hills of the mid-Carolinas), the travel route is little changed. By 1755 the beginning of a "great road", rough but reliable, overlapped the old Catawba Path and was finished as far as Camden. Also, a huge log jam in the Wateree River that had hampered river traffic for many years was cleared, and a private ferry was operating.

After Charleston (Charles Towne) had been established, King George II of England ordered, in 1730, that eleven inland townships for the colonists be founded on the rivers of South Carolina.

That, of course, included the Wateree River, and so in 1732, Camden was founded, a small backcountry settlement at first, later chartered in 1791 thus laying claim as the oldest inland town in the state. Camden, first called Pine Tree Hill, in 1768 was named for Charles Pratt, Lord Camden, who was a British champion of colonial rights. The Camden District Courthouse with one goal (jail) was completed in 1771. At that time the district had only one town, Camden. Today there are nine counties in the same area.

Royal Governor William Campbell had his hands full as he tried to maintain British control of South Carolina. Early in 1775 the South Carolina Province elected their first state governing body to be called "Congress". Men from the Camden District were elected and included Joseph Kershaw for whom the county was later named, and Samuel Boykin, among others. The new governing body drew up a "Declaration of Association" at midyear, pledging to sacrifice their all, even their lives to obtain freedom for South Carolina. Signers included Joseph Kershaw and John Chestnut.

**Map of South Carolina
Districts 1769-1784**

The people of the backcountry (now called the midlands) were on the one hand urged to support the Declaration of Association, and on the other hand to support the loyalists or Tories who swore their allegiance to the Crown.

Baptist clergy did their best to persuade the backcountry men to support the cause of the patriots (rebels, partisans, or Whigs), but converted only a few. This led to the burning of homes and arrests of the "fence sitters" as ordered by Judge William Henry Drayton at Ninety-Six, South Carolina. On September 16, 1775, the backcountry "fence sitters" agreed to remain neutral if assaults on their persons and property would be discontinued. Meanwhile, Governor Campbell dissolved the British Commons House and boarded a British warship in the Charleston Harbor. South Carolina was left to governmental control by the new Provincial Congress.

On December 31, 1775, the British Parliament acted to confiscate the rebelling colonists' land. On March 26, 1776, the members of the South Carolina Congress adjourned and then reconvened as the first General Assembly of South Carolina, electing John Rutledge as President. Joseph Kershaw was a member of the Legislative Council (Senate).

June 28, 1776, brought an attack on Sullivan's Island, South Carolina, by an 11-ship British fleet. Colonel William Moultrie and Colonel William Thompson and their men rebuffed the incursion, and by day's end the British retreated.

Defense of Fort Sullivan in Charleston Harbor

Chapter II

*Is life so dear, or peace so sweet as to be purchased
at the price of chains and slavery?
Forbid it, Almighty God!
I know not what course others may take, but as for me,
give me liberty, or give me death...
-- Patrick Henry, Virginina Convention 1775*

Indenture or Independence

The United States Continental Congress declared Independence from Britain on July 4, 1776. The Revolutionary War had begun.

Meanwhile, in the backcountry of South Carolina, where our ancestors lived, the Cherokee Indians began attacking the settlers with a vengeance. The Cherokee War of 1759-1761, was only the latest uprising of many that had preceded it, but it came at a time when the colonists were also being attacked by other foes at home and abroad. This time, once and for all, the Cherokees were driven back and defeated. They were forced to relinquish their vast South Carolina lands.

After a relatively few years in which the Revolutionary War paid little attention to the South, in 1789, the British turned their focus, first to Georgia, and then to the Carolinas. Charleston was their first target, and the Kershaw District backcountry militia shouldered their response. Sadly, on May 12, 1780, Charleston fell to the British.

Camden and the surrounding areas now became focal points in the war. On June 1, 1780, British General Charles, Lord Cornwallis led his army from Charleston, overland to Camden. Upon the army's arrival the people, waving white flags, surrendered the town. The British immediately occupied the town and established a military post. They took control of all the roads leading into Camden including land and water access to the Wateree River.

For ten months they held the town hostage. The Camden jail figured prominently in the occupation ordeals. The many prisoners of war brought in from other battles as well as local people endured crowded, filthy conditions where illnesses, including smallpox, and dreadful wounds of every description were common. Shortly after (4 days), Cornwallis returned to Charleston leaving Lt. Col. Francis Rawdon in charge.

Rawdon lost no time showing his cruelty and arrogance. He jailed more than 150 men who had to endure the intense heat of summer along with the other jailhouse horrors. Their crime was that they refused to join the British army to fight against their own countrymen. Of course, some citizens accepted the British offers of "protection" rather than go to jail away from their families where they could not help friend or foe.

Prominent citizens arrested were Joseph Kershaw and his brother, Ely. They were shipped as prisoners to Charleston and would have then gone on to British Honduras. However, Ely died of dysentery aboard ship, and Joseph ended up in Bermuda where he sat out the rest of the war.

The Battle of Camden...

Things came to a head in August of 1780. The Continental Congress appointed General Horatio Gates as Commander in the South. Gates was anxious to take away the sting of the fall of Charleston, and he felt he could re-take Camden where only 700 troops held the post. So he gathered together a large army and moved south. Unfortunately, Rawdon became aware of his movements and withdrew all of his troops from outlying posts amassing an army of about 2300 to defend Camden.

On August 16, 1780, at dawn, the two armies engaged. At dawn's early light, the Americans were faced with an army of 3000 as Cornwallis had come up from Charleston to join the fray. The weaker colonials panicked and broke ranks at the sight of the larger enemy, and some ran from the field of battle. Those who remained were out-numbered, and the British soon gained the advantage. The retreating American army suffered a devastating defeat with 900 killed or wounded and 1000 taken prisoner. The British lost only 324. Thereafter it was called "the worst defeat of the war".

Swamp Fox (Francis Marion)

After the Camden loss, ferocious guerrilla actions bedeviled the British with leaders like Francis Marion, "The Swamp Fox", and Thomas Sumter, "The Gamecock", darting in and out of their battle plans and causing untold havoc in the British camps.

May 10, 1781, Rawdon moved out of Camden burning everything in sight as he retreated to Charleston.

There were fourteen notable battles in the area including the Battle of Camden (August 16, 1780), Sanders Creek, Gum Swamp, Hanging Rock, and Hobkirk Hill.

Around 1300 Continental Army troops were killed or wounded. The vicinity of the battles and the ensuing skirmishes prevented the people from returning to their homes until 1781, that is, to any homes that had not been burned by the British.

The British evacuated Charleston to go back to England in December 1782. South Carolina backcountry settlers in the Kershaw County area mostly chose sides in the Revolutionary War and suffered the consequences in so doing. The war destroyed loyalties, lives, and property that many times could not be rebuilt, but the settlers who were left were stronger than ever in their resolve to gain back the justice, freedom, and trust they so badly needed and wanted to form a new nation.

Inland families typically had no slaves. In 1790, the few who did owned fewer than five. But the looming agricultural and economic crisis following the Revolutionary War would cause slavery to be a factor in South Carolina for the next eighty years.

Something else became extremely important to the colonists-Spiritual Renewal. In 1782, local religious meetings were held by Baptist, Presbyterian, and Quaker leaders. Congregations and houses of worship had to be rebuilt as these meeting places fulfilled secular as well as religious functions such as public announcements, the reading of wills, and socializing. White, black, free, slave, male and female all worshiped together in these early meeting houses.

In 1784, Judge William Henry Drayton made a trip to the interior countryside. His journal recorded that the countryside was isolated and desolate. He was traveling from Columbia to Camden and lost his way, returned, hired a guide, and set out again. He described traveling through "pine barren, high and very sandy land", passing "a large circular pond or lake containing 30 acres" (now White Pond), going over "remarkably high ridges", and "reaching gravel near the Wateree River". Drayton gave an account of Revolutionary War destruction. "There are marks of the British having been here. They cut down all the fruit trees and their retreat can be traced by the stacks of chimneys in their wake".

Revolutionary War

The Statue of Freedom
U.S. Capital Dome, Washington D.C.
Thomas Crawford, Artist

 III

If all the world were just,
there would be no need of valor...
-- Plutarch

Freedom and Justice for All

Released from the rule of the British, a new country, the United States of America, set about with earnest the task of restoring and governing the people. They elected their first president, George Washington, who served from 1789-1797. South Carolina became the 8th state to enter the Federal Union known as the United States of America on May 23, 1788.

The first federal population census of the United States occurred in 1790.

An inland settlement like Blaney would not have been attractive except for its proximity to the Wateree River, a major route of transportation, which was first used for commercial and personal travel by way of the Santee to Charleston in 1786.

It seems that some of the first settlers were European families along the Wateree River banks, and they were joined by some Scotch-Irish settlers from North Carolina, Virginia, Maryland, and Pennsylvania. The largest Kershaw County settlement was Scotch-Irish. They built farms on both sides of the Wateree, and, in time, some filtered on southwest of the Wateree to the Lugoff and Blaney area.

Let us not forget that this area was first occupied by native Wateree, Catawba, Congaree, and Cherokee Indians long before colonials arrived, and the Indians did not give up their homeland without a fight. The Indians taught the early settlers how to farm the land, fish, hunt, trade for goods, and showed them travel routes, pottery art, weapon making, medicine cures, and many other life sustaining skills. They also offered lodging for long periods of time in some cases to traveling traders. In fact, the first wealth made in Carolina grew from trading with the Native Americans. The Indians got guns, powder, horses, woven fabrics, colored beads and trinkets, metal knives, axes, and strong drink (rum). The traders got deerskins, hides, foodstuffs, raw materials, handiwork, services, and slaves. The Catawba in particular assumed a peacekeeping role that aided the colonial settlement of Kershaw County. The Cherokee were war-like and scared away many settlers before they got "settled". In many instances the English, French, and Spanish in return gave the Indians European diseases, like smallpox that were deadly to native Americans due to a lack of immunity and treatment.

The Sand Hills, a geographical land barrier of longleaf pines and wire grass well suited to sandy soil, cross what is now Richland, Kershaw, and Fairfield counties. This infertile area of sandy hills and dry arid-like land between the Piedmont and the coastal plains was slowly and sparsely settled from the early days and for a long time thereafter. It is believed that the Sand Hills are a product of what remains of coastal dunes and delta deposits left from a long ago seacoast. The settlers occupied the lower lands first which were more suitable for farming, and the Baptists among them began forming churches in this region.

Some of the Baptist churches formed were Little River in 1768, Spears Creek in 1784, Sandy Level in 1785, Rock Creek in 1792, Beulah in 1806, First of Columbia in 1809, Camden in 1810, Harmony in 1839, Union in 1861, Green Hill in 1863, and Fort Clark in 1870. Methodist churches formed were Smyrna in 1810, and Salem in 1887. Had it not been for Governor Glenn's treaty with the Cherokees in 1755, these churches may never have been established.

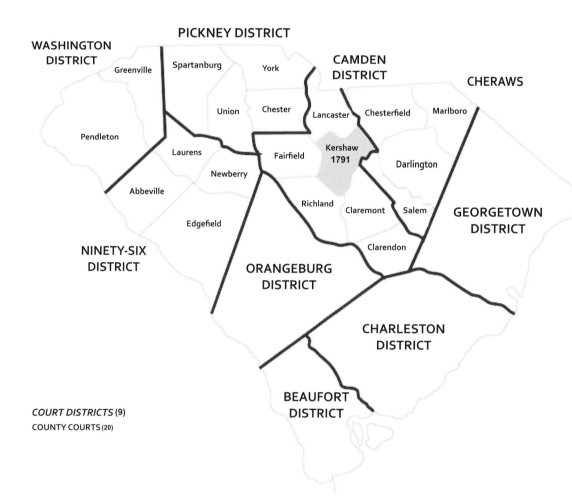

South Carolina Districts 1791-1799

South Carolina Districts 1791-1799. In 1791, Salem County was formed from portions of Claremont and Clarendon counties; and Kershaw County was formed from portions of Claremont, Lancaster, Fairfield, and Richland counties.

Two significant things happened at the end of the 18th Century.
- (1) The invention of the cotton gin by Eli Whitney in 1793.
- (2) The County of Kershaw made its appearance in February 1791.
   The 1800 census showed a total population of 7340 with
   4706 white, 2530 slaves, and 104 other free persons.

   The diary written by Arthur Brown Ross in 1800-1801 gives us an insight into the lives of farmers in the West Wateree area. He was a conductor for the Camden Ferry from the West Wateree side transporting people, mules, cotton, produce, and anything else folks wanted to get across the Wateree River. His wife was Hannah Conger, whom he called his "ole lady". He fished for shad and sturgeon, hunted deer, hogs, bears, turkey, and waterfowl. He made and sold whiskey, tended cattle and hogs and grew flax and cotton for his own use. His social life focused on home and family. He was appointed to the Kershaw County Commission to determine the boundary line between Kershaw County and Fairfield County. He was also appointed in 1785 to Richland County as a Court Justice and was active in many local affairs in that capacity. Arthur Brown Ross described in his Feb.20,1800 diary, the leaving of his son-in law's family for Mississippi in the westward migrations to settle on new land with more fertile soil in unclaimed territory. He recorded, "I heard my daughter cry a quarter of a mile, I think". Five years later, in 1805, Ross and his family also migrated to Mississippi. But that would not be the last of the Ross name in West Wateree, for it would be heard again later in the community of Blaney.

Men polling flatboat 1911 at Peay's Ferry, Courtesy of The Camden Archives

PORTRAIT PROFILE

SAM HENRY ROSS ,SR .
"BUDDY"
10/19/1875 - 9/28/1957

The son of
John Thomas Ross and Mary C. Motley
The husband of Carrie Lee Goff
10/30/1875 - 6/1/1947

CHILDREN
William Fletcher 1897-1939
Ollie Mae
Joseph Paul, Sr. 1901-1980
Mary Elizabeth 1903
Sam Henry, Jr. 1904-1979
Lillie Thelma Knapp 1906
John (Jack) Gary 1908
Katherine Inez 1910
Memphis Woodrow 1912-1988

33 GRANDCHILDREN &
41 GREAT-GRANDCHILDREN

A Blaney-Elgin farmer and merchant with only a second grade education, he owned five general mercantile stores and thousands of acres of land. S. H. Ross General Merchandise was established in Blaney in 1900. He was a faithful member and avid supporter of Union Baptist Church near Elgin, S. C. The church made him Deacon for Life on April 17, 1955, lauding his 38 years as an active deacon. He was a devoted family man and community activist and upon his death left 500 acres of land to each surviving child. He is buried at Union Baptist Church.

Sam H. Ross standing in door of his Blaney store.
Courtesy of Sivas Branham

A More Perfect Union

Truth is a gem that is found at a great depth,
While on the surface of the world
All things are weighed by the false scale of custom…
-- Lord Bryon

The second Baptist church organized in the general territory between Columbia and Camden was Union Baptist Church, established in 1861.

This church, first called Unionville Baptist Church, was started at a very critical time in South Carolina. Its early years were intermingled with war and strife due to the United States Civil War (1861-1865) or as most people know it, "The War Between the States".

The election of Abraham Lincoln as President of the United States in 1861 sent shivers of fear along the spines of many South Carolinians because they believed he would seek to end slavery in the South, and they feared that would destroy their plantation lifestyle and possibly end their very lives and fortunes. The demand for laborers to cultivate cotton, the main southern cash crop, caused the increased slave population. Even though the British had outlawed slavery in 1807 and America closed slave imports from Africa in 1808, the slave population continued to grow. The 1810 census in the Kershaw District showed a total of 9822 persons, 4911 whites and 4832 slaves with 79 other free persons.

By the 1840 census, the Kershaw District had twice the number of slaves (8043) as whites (3988). The 1850 census provided more detailed information in that the census taker listed each individual's name, age, occupation, and race. Race was determined by physical appearance as judged by the census taker. It was found that about half of the free people of color were listed as either black or mulatto. It was important for people of African American heritage to be able to produce proof of freedom to prevent being assumed to be a runaway slave or being sold into slavery. Certificates of freedom were issued by the courts in Camden throughout the antebellum years.

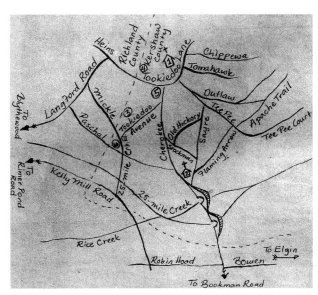

Courtesy of The Blaney-Elgin Museum & Historical Society
Map of Tookiedoo Community

The area west of the Wateree was more thinly settled and had fewer churches that used itinerate preachers traveling through the area. Methodists were active on Sawneys Creek by 1810 and Smyrna Methodist Church was founded by members who had been worshipping at a Fairfield District Church called the Wolf Pit. Another active church with early roots (1840) on 25-mile Creek is Harmony Baptist Church in the Tookiedoo settlement near the present town of Elgin.

Named after a Catawba Indian Chief, Tookiedoo was settled in the early 1600s by the Catawbas who lived and traveled between the Wateree River and the Broad River. Legend says that they built their trading post half way between the two rivers in the area. Citizens commonly find arrowheads in this area. Most of the roads or streets in Tookiedoo have Indian names--Cherokee Blvd., Tomahawk Road, Chippewa Trail, Flaming Arrow Road, and Tee Pee Trail. Others are named for later settlers - Stockman Trail, Paschal Road, and Sayre Lane whose descendents still live in Tookiedoo. No tribal lands were held in Kershaw County during the antebellum period since the Cherokees had ceded all their lands to South Carolina in 1755 and the Catawbas in 1840.

Cureton's Mill…

Court records indicate that the Cureton's Grist Mill and Store began operation in the 1820s on the Rice Creek Springs Road in West Wateree, Kershaw District (Wildwood Lane, Elgin, S. C. today). The grist mill ran from water power as flour, cornmeal, and grits were milled by grinding the various grains and corn between two heavy millstones. People from miles around came by mule and wagon to purchase food and necessities from the store and have their corn and grains ground into flour, grits, and cornmeal. The Mill Store was also used as a West Wateree voting precinct from 1824-1900 (76 years).

In 1861, Unionville Baptist Church was founded near the Cureton Old Mill. In the early days it was common to add "ville" to names of places, towns, or cities in thickly settled communities where a town would likely be located some day. (Example - Sumter was first called Sumterville.)

Cureton's Mill was designated one of eight beats in April 1862 for men organized to patrol the countryside as "Home Guards" in the Kershaw District reserves. James Team coordinated the 1863 Soldiers Board of Relief from the mill store. In 1876 it was a tax collection site as well as the traditional voting place. In late summer of 1878, Kershaw County was a "hot bed" of political intrigue. The Republican Radicals tried to hold a meeting at the mill without letting the Democrats know but were confronted at the meeting with about 75 "red shirts" (former Confederates).

The building of the Seaboard Railroad in 1899-1900 was a time of great change, and thereafter the lives of the people of the Sand Hills were never the same again. The railroad was routed barely two miles from Union Baptist Church (name change in 1881) in confirmation of the Cureton's Mill community influence in locating a train station nearby.

In the 1890s a grade school named Cureton's Mill School was built on Rice Creek Springs Rd. and served the children in the community until the mid 1920s. The school building was later renovated into a dwelling place which the Carl and Bertha Strickland Family acquired and there raised their children, Beecher, Ray, Afon, Nancy, and Tim Strickland. The house was sold around 1953 to Edwin Sessions and was rental property until it was destroyed by fire in 1955. The property located at the intersection of Watts Hill Road and Wildwood Lane is now owned by Steve and Becky McCaskill.

Cureton's Mill was eventually owned and operated by a Captain Rawlins and later still by Jesse Nelson. Nelson's Mill served the Blaney community until the 1930s. It no longer exists today.

Union Baptist Church is still a vital, growing church in the Elgin community today. It is still on the original site on Wildwood Lane at the intersection of Chestnut Road and Smyrna Road .

Bertha Strickland, Curteton's School Building

The Civil War…

By the beginning of the 1850s growing political tensions strained relations between the North and the South. The populace of the Kershaw District was firmly committed to the cotton (known as "white gold") economy and the defense of it, whatever the cost.

South Carolina seceded from the Union on December 20, 1860. Kershaw District residents were ecstatic. Little did they know they were in for four long bloody years of war. All they could envision at the start was giving the "Yankees" a quick lesson in battle strategy to prove their superiority and independence.

Senator James Chestnut immediately resigned his seat in the U. S. Congress when Lincoln was elected president. He returned to South Carolina to help draft South Carolina's Ordinance of Secession. At the Secession Convention in Montgomery, Alabama, Chestnut, Joseph Kershaw, and Thomas J. Withers represented the Kershaw District in organizing the Confederate States of America. Mary Boykin Miller Chestnut's diary recorded, "we have risked all and we must play our best for the stake is life or death."

South Carolina men rushed to form militias made up of rifle clubs or minuteman clubs complete with election of officers, dues, uniforms, meetings, and firearms. In great excitement the men began marching and drilling.

When the federal government attempted to resupply Fort Sumter in Charleston Harbor on April 12, 1861, the Kershaw District militia helped defend the city. At dawn, the battle began with anxious civilians watching from Charleston rooftops. In late afternoon, Union Major Robert Anderson raised a white flag, and everyone there thought, "Well, now the war is over and we can go home." Within a year after the "Battle at Fort Sumter" more than 80% of the entire male population in the Kershaw District above the age of 18 had enlisted.

The Union response was reprinted in the November 1, 1861 *Camden Confederate* newspaper (first issue). The northern *New York Times* newspaper called for vengeance on South Carolina. "Is it not more than poetic justice, that South Carolina, so flagrant in sin, should be made to feel the earliest and heaviest penalties of war? If a southern city must fall, let Charleston be razed to the ground, and salt sowed on its ruins. If southern fields must be desolated by the invasion of Union armies, let South Carolina's cotton and rice plantations be marked by the conquering advances. Let the prayers of Unionists in all 34 states be heard for the early and unsparing chastisement of South Carolina."

Again, South Carolinians felt shivers of fear down their spines mixed with excited anticipation of battles and victories sure to come.

Kershaw District military units were first organized with militias and volunteers, ages 15-50, providing their own weapons, gear, clothing, and horses. They served under local leaders, Gen. Joseph B. Kershaw, Gen. John D. Kennedy, Capt. William Zack Leitner, Capt. Thomas J. Warren, Capt. C. Benton Burns, Capt. Thomas L. Boykin, Capt. Edward McCantey, Capt. R. M. McCantey, Capt. Alexander Hamilton Boykin, Capt. John Chestnut, Capt. William M. Shannon, Capt. James L. Doby, and Capt. Edward M. Boykin. General Wade Hampton of Columbia served state-wide. The Kershaw District Home Guard (reserves) were under the command of Brig. Gen. James Chestnut.

Serving with him were officers Capt. John Thompson and Capt. A. M. Kennedy. The home guards for our area enlisted at Cureton's Mill in West Wateree in 1862. They were to patrol the countryside to keep peace and order and control the slaves. Conscripts began in April 1862 for ages 18-35, in September 1862 for ages 18-45, and in February 1864 for ages 17-50.

At the beginning of the war and for a few months after, there were enough food supplies like sugar, coffee, and tea. Then as the war wore on food supplies got scarce and some ran out completely. People used what substitutes they could find or did without. The bells of Camden churches were used for casting cannon.

In 1844 the invention of the telegraph enabled the first mass communication and President Lincoln took full advantage of this to keep troops and supplies for the troops moving to strategic locations. He also used the far superior railroad lines to transport soldiers and supplies where they were needed most. General Sherman's "scorched earth" march to the sea in the South spelled doom for the Southern cause, but the South was not yet in the mindset to admit defeat.

After Sherman's burning of Atlanta, his movements were closely followed by the home guard in the Kershaw District. On February 17, 1865, Gen. William T. Sherman reached Columbia. That night the sky was aglow with the burning city and Camden prepared to be invaded next. A few days of heavy rain caused the Wateree River to rise to flood stage forcing Sherman to cross higher up the river at Liberty Hill. For more than a week, Sherman's troops remained in the Kershaw District with their onward march hampered by bad weather. They foraged for supplies along the way but found the people had little food or supplies.

On February 23-25, the federal troops commanded by Gen. William B. Hazen destroyed the freight and passenger railroad depots, other railroad property, bales of cotton, government stores, commissary, and rebel army supplies in Camden. The Cornwallis house (used for government storage) was set ablaze. Other stores and cotton sheds were also fired, plus the Masonic Hall and the Wateree Bridge. The soldiers pillaged nearly every house in Camden and Kirkwood.

Union Gen. Edward E. Potter left Georgetown with 2700 white and black troops on April 5, 1865. They entered Camden on April 18 without opposition and broke into the banks and safes first. Since the railroad trains had been moved to Boykin's Mill, they marched there and found the Confederates entrenched. On the morning of April 19, the home guard plus 500 Kentucky cavalrymen met Potter's men at Boykin's Mill. After a brief skirmish the outmanned rebels retreated and disbanded. Since Gen. Robert E. Lee had surrendered more than a week earlier, essentially ending the war, most of the southerners returned to their homes.

By the end of June 1865 the war was over. On June 23 President Andrew Johnson (who assumed the office after Lincoln's assassination) declared an end to the federal blockade that had been in effect for four years. The Kershaw District had paid dearly. Its economy was crippled, infrastructure was in ruins, and hundreds of its people were killed or wounded with lands overrun by invading foes, Gen. William T. Sherman and Gen. Edward E. Potter. During the war years and in the aftermath, hardships prevailed for both those who fought to defend their old lifestyle and those who won their personal freedom from slavery.

Five West Wateree Civil War veterans who died between 1905 and 1928 reached an age of seventy-five plus. C. P. Bowen, a magistrate, died at 64, his 1905 funeral attended by six veterans who were pallbearers. William Branham of Rabons Crossroads reached 85 before his death in 1928. J. J. Bell (75), H. Frank Boykin (77), and Robert Easler (84) all died in 1922. J. J. Bell, a planter, who became the first president of the Bank of Lugoff, had an unusual wartime experience. As a member of Capt. Wheeler's Calvary serving in Georgia, Bell took a Union prisoner who turned out to be Dr. Mary Walker, "the woman surgeon who by Congressional enactment was allowed to appear in male attire". After she was identified, Bell was designated to escort her safely to Union Headquarters.

Civil War 1860 - 1865

Chapter V

The Equality of Pain

Reconstruction in Kershaw County consumed the better part of ten to twelve years, lasting until about 1877. It brought lasting basic changes to all areas of life. A number of issues collided to create an emotional, economic, and political world that was in a free fall making it difficult to survive:

> >Three new amendments to the U. S. Constitution,
> guaranteeing participation of African heritage males in
> politics.
> >Every local government in shambles.
> >Experienced leaders were gone.
> >Agriculture system forever altered by the end of slavery.
> >Farmlands neglected or eroded.
> >Few mules, horses, or work animals.
> >Wateree Bridge destroyed.
> >Roads, telegraph lines, bridges, water channels, railroads,
> damaged or destroyed.
> >Public buildings, mills, homes, barns, fields in ruins.
> >No money to repair or replace anything.
> >Citizens hungry.
> >Mourning lost loved ones and "the lost cause".
> >Trust in fellowman shattered.

The South was put under martial rule. Federal troops arrived in Kershaw County on June 14, 1865. They would stay nine months. They announced to everyone that the slaves were free and took up residence in the Camden City Council chambers and the parks. They did attempt to keep order and encouraged freed slaves to earn their keep. President Andrew Johnson appointed Benjamin Franklin Perry Governor of South Carolina. A convention met on September 13, 1865, in Columbia's First Baptist Church, the same church where secessionists had first convened. Kershaw County's two delegates were Maj. L.W.R. Blair and Col. A.D. Goodwyn, both former Confederates. They repealed the ordinance of secession and acknowledged the freedom of slaves but did not grant African Americans (or women) the right to vote. Office holding was no longer restricted to property owners. The governor was to be elected directly by the people (men only), and he would have veto power. The representative selection by low country parishes was replaced by the district unit for elections to the General Assembly. President Johnson approved the constitution which was not submitted to the state's voters for ratification.

In October 1865, Kershaw County elected former Confederate generals J. B. Kershaw as senator and W. Z. Leitner and W. L. DePass as state representatives. J. D. Kennedy was elected First District representative in the Federal Congress. The new State Legislature met that same month at South Carolina College and their only action was the ratification of the 13th Amendment to the U. S. Constitution, abolishing slavery.

In the Spring of 1866, the U. S. Congress passed the first Civil Rights Act as well as the 14th Amendment to the Constitution upholding the rights of citizens. Parts of the amendment banned former leaders of the Confederate Government from holding state or federal office and punished any state prohibiting an eligible person from voting.

The U. S. Congress ordered a new state constitution be drawn up in 1868 with representatives chosen by the new African American and Caucasian electorate. A convention assembled in January 1868 in Charleston. The Federal Union Republican Party, newly formed by carpetbaggers (Yankee opportunists) and a few South Carolina white scalawags (Southern defectors), controlled the convention. Forty-eight Caucasian men and seventy-six African Americans were sworn in as convention representatives. Of the Caucasians there were only twenty-three native South Carolinians, the other twenty-five were natives of Massachusetts, Ohio, Rhode Island, Connecticut, New York, Pennsylvania, Michigan, England, Ireland, Prussia, Denmark, Georgia, and North Carolina. But, in spite of this diversity, they gave us a good constitution which was used until 1895. It prohibited imprisonment for debt, apportioned representation in the House of Representatives based on the population in a county, provided for a free public school system with compulsory attendance of children between ages 6-16 years, and prohibited lotteries of any kind.

The first election under the new constitution offered a ticket of some of the area's most prominent white men running on the new Democratic Association of Kershaw County Party. Gen. J. B. Kershaw for senator and Col. W.M. Shannon, Dr. E. M. Boykin, and Maj. W. L. DePass for representatives. On the Republican ticket were Senate nominee Justus K. Jillson from Massachusetts (carpetbagger) and House nominees Solomon George Washington Dill from Charleston (scalawag), with two local freedmen, John A. Chestnut and Jonas Nash.

Tensions ran so high that Kershaw County's Provost Marshal Samuel R. Adams wrote a letter on May 16, 1868 to Governor James L. Orr, urging him to send troops to keep the peace.

Elected was the entire Republican field with a slate of two whites and two freedmen gaining control of Kershaw County's delegation, a major change in political power.

Less than a week after Adams's letter to the Governor, Representative Elect S.G.W. Dill was murdered at his home in the Harmony section of western Kershaw County. He was said to have angered local whites with his speeches to freedmen on land distribution, "Forty Acres and a Mule". And due to the fact that he had been a resident of Charleston for 40 years and was a white man seen as turning against his own kind (a Scalawag), he was a hated man. On the night of June 1, 1868, a volley of bullets, shot from the dark into his home, killed Dill and Nester Ray, his armed guard, and wounded Dill's wife.

Federal troops made many arrests, but no evidence was ever found and all suspects were eventually released. Rumors of Ku Klux Klan activity in the area were dismissed as unfounded.

The 1868 elected Kershaw County Delegation was very unusual in that of the four elected, Dill was murdered at his West Wateree residence before taking office, and Jonas Nash died in office causing the need for two special elections. A white man, John H. Boswell replaced Dill and a freedman, William Adamson, succeeded Nash. Senator Justus K. Jillson later became the first South Carolina Superintendent of Education. Only John A. Chestnut was without notoriety.

The 1880s saw the last of the code-of-honor duels so notorious in the South. Duelers were the very men who were law-abiding "pillars of the community", types who were also defenders of their personal honor for real or imagined insults in matters of politics, jealousies and tensions which often led to a rash of duels for a time after the Civil War. Kershaw County was no exception. The last legal duel in Kershaw County occurred on July 5, 1880. It was between E.B.C. Cash and William M. Shannon who met at DuBose's Bridge near Darlington, S. C. Shannon was killed. Both men had served in the Civil War, both had responsible positions in their communities, and both had Kershaw County kin and friends. Cash, grieving the loss of his wife, perceived a slight to her memory as the cause of the offense leading to the duel. Shannon left a wife and thirteen children.

The South Carolina General Assembly passed an enforceable statute against dueling in 1880. It included an oath of office to be taken by all elected office holders in the future. The anti-dueling oath remained in effect until 1947.

In the 1933 Blaney Town election this oath was taken by the newly elected Intendent (Mayor) Samuel Walter Rose and Wardens (Council) J. Paul Ross, William D. Grigsby, Jack G. Ross, and Earl Talmadge Bowen: "I do solemnly swear before God and those present to discharge the duties of the office to which I have been elected faithfully, honestly, and impartially. Also to defend the law and ordinances of the Town of Blaney, State of South Carolina and the United States of America, and shall not engage in or assist in any manner in a duel".

The late 1800s were a time of unusual gun violence, and the South Carolina General Assembly in 1897 confounded many by reducing penalties for violating the concealed weapons law, which actually encouraged the carrying of weapons. With the history of gun deaths during the two decades preceding the "Great War", it appears that many citizens carried weapons.

At war's end, the newly freed slaves were under the assumption that they would be given allotments of enough land and implements to be self-supporting. Whites naturally were afraid their land would be given to former slaves. South Carolina was the only southern state to benefit freedmen with a land distribution plan and it did not include taking land from the whites. In 1869 the South Carolina Land Commission was given an appropriation to buy large tracts at public expense and to resell lots at low cost and lenient terms to the homeless poor of both races. In Kershaw County 6,360 acres of land was bought for the land distribution. However, much of the land was said to have been exhausted or eroded and not fertile enough for farming. Also it was revealed that the Land Commission had paid more for the land than it was worth, thus squandering hard earned public tax money.

The historian Carol Bleser states, "The history of the Land Commission during 1869-72 is an example of the moral slump that was characteristic of government at all levels during the Grant era." The Republican administration of U.S. President Ulysses S. Grant, 1869-77, is viewed by historians as marked by scandal, graft, and a general decline in ethics in government.

Glimmers of light showed through the Reconstruction darkness in 1872 when the *Camden Journal* reported on the progress of the new free bridge being built by J. B. LaSalle over the Wateree River. The people rejoiced in the news reported by the *Kershaw Gazette* on Feb. 3, 1872, that "The Bridge Commissioners having in charge the building of the free bridge across the Wateree River, report that they have accomplished the work and it is a sound and substantial structure."

SAMUEL WALTER ROSE
1/24/1867 - 7/3/1949

The son of John Walter Rose and Mary Elizabeth Watts
The husband of Dossie G. Percival & Elizabeth Percival
CHILDREN - (Dossie)
Walter English, Lillie Rose, Jessie G., Leslie Coliva
Mary, John Gillard, Mattie Edith, Arlin Chester
CHILDREN - (Elizabeth)
Elise, Stanley Norman, Lillie, Fannie

>Born in Richland County.
>1938, 1947-1948 - Intendent (Mayor) of Blaney, S. C.

Samuel Walter Rose was a farmer but he and his family resided in the town of Blaney. They lived on the corner of Rose and Main Street across from where the Elgin Town Hall is today. Charlie Wray Wooten and his wife Willie Mae Wooten were his neighbors. Maude and Alton Nelson also lived nearby. Town Hall records are sketchy for the early days of the town's existence and it is possible that he served as Mayor longer than present records indicate. From 1908 until 1967 Intendents (Mayors) served one year terms. Records available indicate he was very interested in town arrests and often paid the fines for those deserving help.
He is buried at Union Baptist Church Cemetery.

The election of 1872 was boycotted by many outnumbered white voters. A local report on Oct. 24 stated that Cureton's Mill in West Wateree had opened for a general election only once since the war and did not open for this election. The Republican Regulars were comfortably re-elected. The Sumter scalawag, Franklin J. Moses, Jr., was elected Governor of South Carolina. He had been associated with the Kershaw County land fraud and was called "the robber governor". Wade Hampton, in Columbia, called for southern whites to "dedicate themselves to the redemption of the South."

Violence erupted in the 1876 election campaign between the incumbent Governor Daniel Henry Chamberlain and his opponent, Wade Hampton. Many acts of suspected or admitted arson on both sides aimed at Caucasian and African American citizens were the order of the day. Chamberlain requested federal troops be sent to South Carolina, and on October 17, President Grant sent a troop of 29 enlisted men and four officers to Camden where Hampton was to speak. The *Kershaw Gazette* reported a torchlight parade of 5000 men escorted Hampton to the speaker's platform in the town square, thereafter known as Hampton Square (Hampton Park today). Hundreds of men from all over the countryside and neighboring counties vocalized their support.

By comparison, Kirkland and Kennedy write, that when Chamberlain came to Camden to speak, tension and fear arose as hordes of African Americans packed the streets, and a great number of mounted Red Shirts, composed of many white Confederates, defiantly rode among them. A state of uproar, confusion, and terror ruled for hours. President Grant also ordered all southern white gun clubs and hunting clubs to disband. They did, and then reorganized into "music clubs" or "baseball clubs", mounted, of course. They also continued to wear Red Shirts.

There were many "irregularities" in the 1876 election. Voters were sent from "poll to poll" trying to find an open poll. Voters were intimidated and some ballot boxes never made it to the place where they were to be counted. Red shirted men were "ever-present", and some rode from "poll to poll", voting at each poll. But in the end, Hampton "won" by a little more than 1000 votes. The county went into "overdrive" as men celebrated his victory.

Chamberlain would not concede the election, and both sides claimed victory. When Hampton and his supporters arrived at the State House, they were met by federal troops and retired to another location. For four months there were two rival governments in South Carolina.

In the nation's capitol, the Republican Rutherford B. Hayes had defeated Democrat Samuel Tilden by just one electoral vote. A special "election committee" awarded all 22 disputed votes (seven from South Carolina) to Hayes when any one of which would have given the presidency to Tilden. Democrats were furious and swore to block Hayes's inauguration. The Republicans, who were eager to spend four more years in power, offered compromises. They would subsidize southern railroads and withdraw the last of the federal troops from Florida and South Carolina. And thus, Reconstruction ended and the way was cleared for native citizens to reclaim their government. Hayes was inaugurated without incident and, convinced that Hampton, not Chamberlain, controlled the state, ordered federal troops to leave on April 3, 1877. On April 11, Chamberlain withdrew from the State House…and Hampton moved in.

Eli Whitney had invented the cotton gin in 1793 and cotton was planted as a good money crop for years. At the turn of the century in 1900 it became known as King Cotton, the farmers' main cash crop. Blaney farmers brought bags and bags of cotton to gins in mule or horse- drawn wagons during harvest season. They transported their cotton over the Wateree River on a ferry in all kinds of weather and floods to get to the nearest gin. Unfortunately, planting cotton year after year quickly depleted the soil's fertility, so more fields were needed, and more labor to clear added fields was required.

With federal Reconstruction over, Kershaw County could move out of one of the most chaotic times in its history. A stabilizing white power was again in control, no enemy army was present, and the unknown future looked promising for one and all. Even the future of the ever-flood-prone Wateree Bridge looked bright, for in 1883 a new steel toll bridge was constructed in a better location, ready for the new century's challenges.

PORTRAIT PROFILE

The son of
Thomas H. Griffin Jeffers
2/2/1840 - 9/4/1868
and
Tina Carolina Ross
8/14/1834 - 2/3/1910
The Husband of
Mary Elizabeth Goff

CHILDREN
Bernice Corinna Jeffers Nelson
3/31/1894 - 6/29/1986
William D. 1896, Thomas C. 1897
Attie 1899, Furman 1901, Dothan E. 1904
and Mamie G. 1907

WILLIAM THOMAS JEFFERS
12/30/1863 - 11/18/1915

He was the first postmaster and a farmer in the Blaney community which was first called Jeffers. The Jeffers Post Office was established in 1898 in his home on Blackjack Street, and he delivered the mail on horseback north to Killian and south to English. In 1899 he served Union Baptist Church near Blaney-Elgin as Church Clerk. He loved to sing in church and also served as a deacon at Union Baptist Church. His story as a farmer, postmaster, and family man was recalled by his daughter Bernice, so we would know today that Mr. Jeffers was instrumental in paving the way for Blaney's birth as a prosperous town at the turn of the century. He is buried at Union Baptist Church near Elgin, S. C.

Logan and Bernice Jeffers Nelson

Blaney Depot 1908
Courtesy of Blaney - Elgin Museum & Historical Society

 VI

Not unless we fill our existence with an aim
Do we make it life.
--Reichel

The Railroad to the Future

The Civil War and the Reconstruction years made it hard for the people, of what we now call the midlands in South Carolina, to make any significant headway toward organizing into towns. But the Blaney community had a slight advantage in that it was situated 24 miles north of the capitol city of the state, Columbia, on U. S. Highway #1, (the Capitol Highway), and about eight miles from the very important waterway, the Wateree River, and a few more miles to the north was the town of Camden, the Kershaw County seat. The Blaney community originally had one road intersection known by many names, Jeffers, Simpson, Ross, and Rose.

The people of the Blaney rural community, once considered the "lost territory", were primarily farmers who had built up their lands, improved their orchards, established new churches, and grew cotton (their main cash crop), grain, corn, peas, and potatoes. Farmers cut cross ties for cash income during the winter and buyers came each week to buy them loaded on rail cars. Trees were available and plentiful due to land clearing for farming. Some citizens were merchants, saw millers, grist mill operators, physicians, teachers, tenants, and some found a new profession, at least for the Blaney community, as railroad workers.

In 1899-1900, the Seaboard Air Line Railroad constructed by the Southbound Railroad Co. made its way across the midlands of South Carolina. Construction began at Cayce on July 1, 1899, and was completed to Camden on May 10, 1900. By 1901, the Seaboard Railroad had constructed a steel trestle across the Wateree River, making the trip from Columbia to Camden only one and a half hours long. Dating from 1824, stage coach travel took several days each way. When the tracks came through the southwest corner of Kershaw County, the workers were lodged in a two-room crudely-built section house beside the railroad in the community of Blaney, which was called Jeffers at that time. The section house was on property later owned by Thomas W. Watson who built a home around it in 1906.

The economic impact of the arrival of the railroad cannot be overstated. The depot at Blaney was the pivotal source for the evolution of the community with commerce coming in and going out on a regular basis. The railroad route came from northern cities to depots in Cheraw, Bethune, Cassatt, Shepherd, Camden, Lugoff, and Blaney. The early wood-burning locomotives required many stops to get fuel and water. The communities with depots thrived with commerce, mail, freight, and passenger service. Post offices, boarding houses, restaurants, warehouses, general stores, banks, churches, and schools were built or enlarged in these economic centers.

When the construction of the railroad and depot started at Blaney, tents sprang up everywhere, and water was drawn from the household well of Mr. William Thomas Jeffers. The green coffee was roasted and then ground from the coffee mill set up along side the Jeffers house, and Mr. Jeffers, with the help of his wife, Mary Elizabeth Goff, provided a little commissary for the workers to buy food.

Mrs. Bernice Corinna Jeffers Nelson (the oldest daughter of William Thomas Jeffers, born March 31, 1894) recalls that Blaney was first called Jeffers because, "my father (Mr. Jeffers) had the first post office in our house on Blackjack Street. He was the mail carrier and postmaster too. (Mr. William T. Jeffers was appointed the first postmaster in 1898). He carried the mail on horseback as far north as Killian and ten to twelve miles south to English, way back down in the country." She said, "My mother, Mary Elizabeth, begged my father to give up the mail route because it was too hard on both of them."

When Lindsay Guy built a store in Blaney, the post office moved there, and Mrs. Nelson's uncle, Jesse T. Ross, became the postmaster on June 29, 1900 and served until his retirement on July 31, 1946 (46 years). After the railroad came through, the mail was brought by train. Outgoing mail was hung on a stationary crane. As the train came by, an arm was extended out from the train to catch the mail bag. Mind you, the train was traveling about 50-70 miles per hour.

Lawrence D. Evans was the first mail carrier. He delivered the mail in a horse and buggy, and you could hear him coming by his distinctive whistling a long time before he actually got to your house. His mail route mileage was measured by the number of buggy wheel turns. Walter L. Miles followed him next and carried the mail for a long time. Then Boykin K. Rose was the mail carrier.

Mr. W. T. Jeffers and his brother Joe Jeffers opened another general merchandise store, and Mr. Sam Henry Ross and Mr. Jim Cooper also opened stores in Blaney. These stores and all other business activity for the community were located on Main Street, which is now called Church Street, which was and still is located near the railroad tracks. The railroad was a great help in keeping these stores stocked with food and other merchandise for sale. The people, especially the farmers, relied on the railroad to keep them supplied with life's necessities.

The name of the developing community first called Jeffers was changed to "Blaney" in honor of a New York banker by that name who had been instrumental in funding the railroad as a stockholder and was a Vice President of the Seaboard Air Line Railroad. The name Blaney was made official when the town was chartered and incorporated on January 23, 1908.

Mrs. Nelson's mother and father had a farm in the fields beyond their house. "We didn't have much to sell. Daddy grew cotton, corn, peas and potatoes, but we didn't have much of it. Daddy had a whole lot of trees cut and began to plant more cotton. They had a market for it in Camden. I remember going to that mill (Cureton's or Nelson's) out there in the country to have corn ground. That was the best kind of bread."

Mrs. Bernice Nelson also remembered, "two slavery women and one man who worked for her parents. They said that White Pond used to be right below her father's house, but a big hole appeared in the ground and all the water left and came up in the place where White Pond is today. Then from this White Pond there sprang up another pond called Black Pond". Facts tell us that the private White Pond has been on maps since the 1800s and is a local landmark. It is a natural pond believed to lack sufficient "in-flow". There is no visible inlet or outlet. Legend says it is "bottomless". In times of drought it is often low or dry. Today it is two miles east outside the Town of Elgin limits off White Pond Rd.

On the left, President Dwight David Eisenhower
at White Pond
Courtesy of Wayne Nelson

Mrs. Nelson stated that "Momma and Daddy were church-going people. My daddy was Superintendent of Sunday School at Ridgeside first, and then joined Union Baptist Church where he and his brother, Joe Jeffers were made deacons. Uncle Joe led the singing at Union Church and my daddy, William Thomas Jeffers, sang bass, with my Momma, Mary Elizabeth Jeffers, singing tenor."

She talked about how funerals were conducted in those days, saying that they were different from today. "Henry Ross and Jim Dawkins were the community gravediggers. Most people had to walk wherever they went in those days, including funerals, and so usually the funerals were not well attended. Most funerals were very short with only a few verses of scripture and a song. Since they had no song books, a stanza would be recited for the people to sing afterward. That was how folks learned their hymns in those days. Graves were not marked by elaborate tomb stones, only a simple marker or stone would do."

Time seemed to stand still in the Blaney community. For years water came from the community well which was 125 feet deep. Later Mr. John Kirkland put in a small water system. Mrs. Nelson recalled, "I had two or three children when I saw my first car, around 1916 or so. Uncle Simon Ross got the first, but it was a long time before they paved any roads around here. It was hard to drive the sandy roads in the community because you could turn over real easy."

Mrs. Bernice Nelson told that when she was a child going to school, the trains would stop at the depot to unload materials and load farm goods to be sold. "We'd be late for school sometimes, and we used to crawl under the train when it stopped. We did that so we wouldn't be late. Yea, it was dangerous, but we did it."

Blaney home-circa 1905 - Main Street,
Photo by Judy Darby-Buchanan

PORTRAIT PROFILE

JOHN PHILLIP ISENHOWER
8/20/1870 - 8/18/1964

The son of
Martha Stuart and John Isenhower
of
Fairfield County

First Blaney Intendent
(Mayor)
1/23/1908

>Educated at Furman University and ordained as a Minister of the Gospel of Jesus Christ, Sept.
  17, 1896. Served as Pastor in Richland, Kershaw, and Fairfield Counties in S. C.
>Taught Public School 1896 - 1901.
> Pastor of Blaney Baptist Church, Blaney, S. C.
  1904 as a missionary - unfinished church building occupied.
  1905 organized into a church at a salary of $100 per year.
  1906-1908 - Recalled as Pastor. Church building completed in 1908.
>January 23, 1908 - Elected the first Intendent (Mayor) of Blaney, S. C.
>Pastor of Union Baptist Church, Blaney, S. C.
  January 1908 with salary of $50 per year to preach once monthly.
  April 3, 1909 - Called for another year.
  Reorganized Sunday School and placed wire fence around cemetery.
  Proposed uniting Blaney and Union Churches.
>Moderator of Fairfield Baptist Association 1914-1927.
>President of Wateree Baptist Association 1922.
>Member of the South Carolina Legislature 1927-1930; 1933-1936, 1945

Buried in Mount Olivet Cemetery, Ridgeway, S. C.
Fairfield County, S. C.

1908 Blaney Incorporation…

A petition was filed with the Secretary of State of South Carolina on November 27, 1907, by ten freehold electors in the Blaney precinct setting forth the corporate town limits, the number of inhabitants, and a request that they be incorporated as a town. A commission was issued to Jesse Thomas Ross, William Thomas Jeffers, and James Belton Cooper empowering them to provide for the registration of all electors within the corporate limits of the town, to appoint managers to hold the election, and to certify the results to the Secretary of State.

R.W.J. Kennedy, J. D. Faust and J. W. Bradley were appointed managers of election, and they set an election date for the purpose of determining the incorporation of the town of Blaney for January 23, 1908.

The election was held on January 23, 1908, and the electors within the so designated town limits voted to incorporate the town to be named Blaney. They also elected the first Intendant (Mayor) and four Wardens (Council).

Rev. John Phillip Isenhower was elected Intendant. Rev. Isenhower was 38 years of age and the part-time pastor of both Blaney Baptist Church and Union Baptist Church in the community.

Elected as Wardens (Council) were James Belton Cooper, B. B. Crisp, R.W.J. Kennedy, and T. M. McCaskill.

The Secretary of State issued the Certificate of Incorporation of the Town of Blaney on January 23, 1908, in the 132nd year of the Independence of the United States of America.

As an aside, the President of the United States in 1908 was Theodore Roosevelt, and Charles Fairbanks was the Vice President.

The South Carolina Governor elected in the General Election on November 3, 1908, was Democrat Martin Frederick Ansel who won a second 2-year term without opposition with 61,060 votes.

The U. S. Senate election started with a democratic primary on Aug. 25 and a run-off on Sept. 8 between "Cotton Ed" Smith and John Gary Evans with Smith the winner with 69,318 to Evans's 39,656 votes. Subsequently the S. C. General Assembly elected Smith to a 6-year term. This election was prior to the 17th Amendment to the U. S. Constitution when U. S. Senators were elected by the state legislature and not through direct election by the people of the state.

Ellison D. Smith, an official of the Cotton Association and often called "Cotton Ed", entered the Democratic primary but found himself in early trouble when he promised that cotton would rise to 18 cents and it did not occur. However, his rhetorical skills gave him command of the stump speeches in the state and attracted many voters to his campaign. Former Governor J. G. Evans was making his 4th straight attempt for the U. S. Senate seat and had received the support of Senator Ben Tillman. The tide of Tillmanism had receded in the state, and Tillman's endorsement doomed Evans's prospects. In the run-off/face-off, Evans once again failed to carry the day, and "Cotton Ed" Smith scored a resounding victory.

In the November general election seven U. S. House of Representatives were selected for 2-year terms. All seven were re-elected, and the state delegation remained solely Democratic.

1st District -   George Swinton Legare`

2nd District -James O' H. Patterson

3rd District - Wyatt Aiken

4th District -   Joseph T. Johnson

5th District -   David E. Finley

6th District -   J. Edwin Ellerbe

7th District -   Asbury Francis Lever

The number of congressional districts in 1908 was determined by the results of the 1900 Census. There have been as few as four and as many as nine districts over the years.

Thelma Knapp at Sam H. Ross Store
Courtesy of Sivas Branham

School Days…

You may be interested in the school systems in Kershaw County at the turn of the 20th Century. The first known school was Ridgeside, a one-room log house which would be at the corner of Miles and Steven Campbell Roads today. The teacher was Mr. Harold Morrell. Later a three-room school was built. In 1889 Mr. McMahan was the Kershaw County Supt. of Education, and there were 26 segregated school districts.

Year Term	System	Schools	Teachers	Students	Budget
1901	white	58	66	2690	$13,735.00
	black	49	53	2974	4,859.00
1930	white 165 day	19consolidated	40+	2311	
	black 86 day	49	82	5487	

The Blaney School District #12

Year	System	1-Room School	Teachers	Students	Term
1900	white	3	3	73	84 day
	black	2	2	82	84 day

1885--S. C. instituted the modern graded school system of specific standards to pass from grade to grade.

1900-1950 white schools	**Blaney, graded & high, Concord, Crescent, Cureton's Mill, Harmony, Lugoff Ridgeside (ville), Sand Hill, Trinity**	
1900-1950 black schools	**Blaney, Green Hill, Fort Clark, Concord Jackson graded & high, Lugoff, Smyrna, Wateree, Weeping Mary**	

Blaney School Highlights:
1907 - Blaney School library established.
1913 - 3-Room/ 3-Teacher/8th Grade school/117 pupils/100 day term.
1915 - New brick school built for $8000.00.
1916 - C. G. Williams principal of 244 pupil school.
1920 - Compulsory education in county, not enforced.
1930 - E. W. Rentz principal of 12 teacher staff/l65 day term.
1931 - New brick 2-story Blaney Graded & High School. (Had 11-17 graduates each year.)
       Black students to Jackson Graded & High School in Camden

The comparison between the 1931 Blaney High School and the 1900 one-room school reveals the growth of the Blaney community and the Kershaw County Education Program. The population of the town of Blaney in the 1910 census was 115. In the 1930 census it was 175. The schools were attended by all the community children, not just by those from the town.

Trinity School District #11 (Hwy 34, Ridgeway Rd., and Smyrna Rd.)
Mrs. Lois Branham Carns of Smyrna Rd., Elgin, SC, related that some of her older brothers attended this school, always walking to school.
1900 - white system   4 schools/4 teachers/158 pupils/96 day term.
1913 - 2 room/2 teacher/10 grades/69 pupils/140 day term.
1916 - N. P. Gettys, principal - 92 student school with wagon to carry 16 students @$120 per term. Library of 150 books.

1910 CENSUS OF THE TOWN OF BLANEY
25 Households of 62 Adults and 53 Children
Three unpaved streets named: Blackjack Street, Main Street, and West Avenue

Occupations:

9 Farmers	Wm. T. Jeffers, Wm. D. Hinson, Alonzo Bowen, Ed M. Flaridy, Lewis Hinson, Wm. J. Harley, Wm. J. Motley, Alfred E. Gunter, John W. Bradley
1 Physician	William D. Grigsby
4 Merchants	Jesse T. Ross, Lewis Sharpe, Thomas W. Watson, and James B. Cooper
1 Postmaster	Jesse T. Ross
1 Mail Carrier	Lawrence D. Evans
1 Depot Agent	Robert L. Vick
1 RR Section Master	George T. Heavener
1 Blacksmith	George Glover
1 RR Laborer	Foster Hutton
9 Home Farm Laborers	(young single men)
1 Real Est. Agent	Richard W. Sutton
2 Teachers	Zoie Bailey, Blanche W. Harley
3 Cooks	Daisy Brown, Mosely Tillman, Laura Watkins
1 Boarding House Mgr.	Helen M. Bailey
1 Woodyard Foreman	Fletcher Faust
5 Adult Farm Laborers	

   The finding of the March 4, 1913 survey map of the Town of Blaney, S. C., gives us insight into the early configuration of the fledgling community. The survey was made at the request of Jesse T. Ross, Intendent (Mayor),and Wardens (council members) W. F. Duke, J. G. Feaster, W. L. Miles, and T. W. Watson. The map shows an area of 217.3 acres and locates the Capitol Highway, Seaboard railroad, Blaney Church, Blaney School, and the J. T. Ross store/post office. J. T. Buvekue was the Engineer/Surveyor.

PORTRAIT PROFILE

The son of
Rev. Brown C Ross and Mary Ann Moak
12/22/1831 - 11/28/1893
and
12/26/1845 - 12/14/1926

the husband of
Nancy E. (Nannie) Goff & Georgia W. Bishop
(9/7/1876 - 1/19/1936

CHILDREN - (Nannie)
Ellerbe Hazel 1898 - 1986
Charlotte E. 1900 - 1961
Willis 1902 - & Willoughby 1902 - 1976
Monnie Elouise 1904 - 1922
Nellie R. 1906 -1908
Zelma Beatrice Hamlin 1909 - 1993
Ethel M. 1912 - 1913
Jessie T., Jr. 1915
10 Grandchildren and 15 Great-Grandchildren

JESSE THOMAS ROSS
7/271876 - 10/31/1959

>1900-1946- Postmaster at Blaney, S. C.
>Member of Union Baptist Church, Blaney, S. C. at early age.
>1903-Gave two acres of land to build Blaney Baptist Church, joined the church, and helped
   organize.
>1905-Elected Blaney Baptist Church Clerk and Treasurer.
>1905-A farmer, he owned and operated a General Merchandise Store on Main Street in Blaney,
   S. C.
>1909-1915 - Elected Intendent (Mayor) of the Town of Blaney, S. C.
> Member of Ancient Free Masons and Knights of Pythias.
> Blaney Schools Trustee - 25+ years.

   Jesse Thomas Ross returned to Union Baptist Church for the last six years of his life. He gave
$1000 to the Union Building Fund on a remodeling of the church building. He presented the
church with a new Hammond organ in 1958 in memory of his father, Rev. Brown C. Ross who
was their first pastor. He donated new hymnals to the church and made many other contributions.
He is buried at Union Baptist Church.

Progress or Not...

Sometimes progress brings change that is not wanted. In the Town of Blaney it became necessary to purchase locks for doors that previously had been unlocked, and night watchmen were hired to "guard" the stores, warehouses, lumber yards, and other businesses. In 1913, two arson fires destroyed two stores and all the contents, and then just 10 days later the Railroad Depot and contents were lost. Finding the guilty parties was just about impossible as the town had no police or fire department yet.

Blood was shed in another incident brought on by a heated discussion of politics in September 1912. Lon Bowen and Thomas Sessions and his son, Lewis were the participants as reported by the *Columbia Record* newspaper. They were discussing the 1876 election between Governor Chamberlain and Gen. Wade Hampton of Columbia. Bowen had a brick and Sessions a knife, and things might have gotten totally out of hand had Charles Hall, a bystander, not knocked the knife out of Sessions's hand. The *Columbia Record* reporter concluded, "While blood was spilled and blows given and taken, the battle of the '76 election remains as unsettled as ever."

State politics was in a "sorry state" during the Governor Coleman L. Blease term of office (1/17/1911-1/14/1915). He granted 1624 pardons and paroles and disbanded the state militia leaving the state unprotected for weeks among other outrageous acts. Impeachment looming, he resigned January 14, 1915. Lt. Governor Charles A. Smith was sworn in 10 minutes later. He served only five days before leaving office.

Of note in the county seat, in November 1905 a new courthouse building graced the landscape in Camden, and it cost only $25,000.

Camden to Lugoff-Blaney on west side of the Wateree River 1916
Courtesy of The Camden Archives

In December 1913, a wealthy Wall Street financier, Bernard Baruch, gave $5000 for land and $25,000 for building the Camden Hospital at the corner of Fair and Union Streets. He was the son of a Civil War surgeon, Dr. Simon Baruch, who practiced medicine in Camden for fifteen years after the war. Baruch, born in Camden, moved to New York in 1880. It was intended to be a hospital for all the citizens in Kershaw County. It was to be a 20-bed facility with one ward for Caucasians and one for African Americans, with operating rooms in between the wings. They purchased the old Presbyterian manse and property and used it for the administration building with reserved space for several private rooms for paying patients. Some free patients were to be accepted using local funds. The patient cost per day was $2.64.

Floods and Bridges...

The story of the Wateree River, its ferries, bridges, and floods is "very interesting" to say the least. Ferries were used until the first wooden covered toll bridge was built over huge stone piers by the Camden Bridge Co. in 1828, called the Ithiel Town bridge. Only wagons loaded with cotton could cross free. This bridge was destroyed by an 1831 flood. The use of ferries was necessary from 1831 to 1838 when a second bridge was built only to be damaged in 1854 and then destroyed by fire in the Civil War by Sherman's Union troops in 1865. Ferries then had to be used until 1874. The J.B. LaSalle free wooden bridge lasted from 1874 to 1877 when it was declared a dangerous bridge and was destroyed by the county. This bridge was replaced by an "iron toll bridge" in a changed location in 1883. The King Bridge Co. raised this bridge 5 ft. above floodwater level in 1902 at a cost of $15,000. Henry Savage, Sr., a bridge company executive, oversaw the bridge construction.

1910 Wateree free bridge destroyed by 1916 flooding
Courtesy of The Camden Archives

But the floodwaters rose to new unheard of heights in the 1908 flood that completely washed out the 1883 Savage Bridge. It had been raining for two days prior to the wash-out, and many trees and other debris were brought downstream in the flood. Henry Savage was standing on the bridge directing some men trying to clear the debris. When the bridge broke apart, the men working to dislodge debris under the bridge were tossed into the raging water. Savage too went into the water and was rescued 10 miles downstream clinging to driftwood. Mr. George Rabon and a boy named Hinson were on the bridge in a wagon when the bridge collapsed. They were never seen again. Five people were lost in total and believed dead. Two workers were also rescued after clinging to trees all night in the flood. The next day the river was measured at 39 ft. 7 inches. Roads south and east were impassable. Forty ft. of the Columbia road were washed out. It was back to the ferries again from 1908 to 1910.

On September 15, 1910, a new free-to-traffic steel bridge opened with great fanfare at a cost of $40,000 in borrowed money due to be paid back by Kershaw County in twenty-five years.

On July 18, 1916, after two days of steady rain, floodwaters reaching a record 40.4 ft. washed out the steel bridge with 19 years of payments left on the county bridge debt. The Seaboard Railroad trestle with coal filled gondolas was also lost. Three workers for the railroad perished when raging river currents swept them away. There were damaged crops, loss of livestock and timber, and people stranded on top of houses and in trees. The single telegraph and telephone wire between Camden and Richmond was washed out of commission.

The dams needed in the Catawba-Wateree River System to stop the flooding had been in the planning stage since 1904 when the Wateree Dam site was purchased. The 1908 and the 1916 disastrous floods made progress more urgent to prevent future losses of precious lives and property. In 1916 the ferry was back in business at 25 cents per vehicle and 10 cents for each passenger.

Some West Wateree cotton farmers in the Trinity School community called a meeting of all West Wateree farmers to discuss the "demoralized cotton market" as described by the *Camden Chronicle* in 1914. The group agreed that selling their cotton for the current 6 or 7 cents would "ruin the farmer and take 5-6 years to recover". They also agreed to sell no cotton until they met again at the end of October to assess the cotton situation before adopting a course of action. One of the problems affecting the cotton market was the warring conflict of nations in Europe. Millions of bales of cotton lay unsold because of the war and, coupled with the weather variances, presented a sizable hurdle that would not be overcome in the near future.

Chapter VII

The Great War

Oh, East is East. and West is West,
And never the twain shall meet,
Till Earth and Sky stand presently
At God's great Judgment Seat.
But there is neither East nor West,
Border, nor Breed, nor Birth,
When two strong men stand face to face,
Tho; they come from the ends of the Earth!
--Rudyard Kipling

On April 2, 1917, President Woodrow Wilson requested the Congress to declare war between the United States and Germany. They did so on April 6, 1917, entering the war after almost three years of war overseas. Although the combat period was short - Spring 1917 to Fall 1918, the war actually helped the local economy grow (as wars often do). Vacations and tourism increased in South Carolina while it decreased in Europe as many Europeans escaped war turmoil for more peaceful shores.

The downsides, however, were many. Kershaw County soldiers had to go to war in Europe leaving their families to cope on their own. Cotton farmers were unable to prepare for the boll weevil damage already suffered in Georgia and headed their way. The Wateree Bridge which was washed out and destroyed in 1916 had not been replaced, and since a large debt remained from the previous bridge it was not likely to be replaced in the foreseeable future. Shortages of materials and financing a new bridge proved an almost insurmountable hurdle. Work could not proceed on the dam needed to corral the Wateree River due to a shortage of manpower between demands for war and dam construction work.

Company M First Infantry Regiment, Kershaw County National Guard. Camden Armory 1916
Courtesy of The Camden Archives

The Kershaw County National Guard, Company M, left from the Seaboard train station for the war effort just 10 days after war was declared. The all white company had just returned in December 1916 aboard the Seaboard Railroad from an unsuccessful incursion over the Mexican Border, commanded by Gen. John J. Pershing, pursuing PanchoVilla for his raids into America.

There was a lot of praise for President Woodrow Wilson who had been brought up as a boy in Columbia, S. C. Both blacks and whites answered the draft in large numbers. In Blaney they registered for the draft at the Blaney Post Office. In Kershaw County 2400 men registered. The African American soldiers left separately for segregated training at Camp Jackson, though for the first time both African American and Caucasian men were to serve together for national defense.

The area was not only proud of President Wilson and the fact that more than half of the American Army would be trained in the South, but they backed Bernard Baruch, a Camden native, who was handling the supplies needed by the armies and the war effort.

The home front was not left completely unprotected as men as young as 16 and other undrafted men and women responded to the needs at army posts, protecting vital bridge and railway trestles and other patrol duties.

The need for more food production galvanized many in the county to grow more corn and wheat. The dangerous, expensive, much needed Wateree Dam project which lasted far longer than "The Great War" was finally over. The destructive power of the Wateree River was tamed on September 14, 1919, as Southern Power Company and the Hardaway Construction Company flipped the switches transmitting 100,000 horsepower into a general power circuit. The half-mile dam across the Wateree River had employed hundreds of men and created a lake 20 miles long at a cost of $6,000,000. No one at the time realized just how much this would change forever the lives of the entire region. The long wait for the replacement Wateree Bridge came to an end on February 3, 1920, and it was a blessing even though it was a wooden toll bridge that charged 50 cents for automobiles and 5 cents for mule teams.

The end of the war loomed when the government took over the railroads to move massive numbers of men and machines. Spanish influenza of epidemic proportions and highly contagious affected Kershaw County citizens in October 1918. All ages and communities were afflicted. Schools and churches were closed and mills ceased work. All public gatherings were cancelled. More than 600 were treated in the county while 195,000 Americans fell ill. More people died of the flu than died in "The Great War". Kershaw County lost 49 in the war, 24 African Americans and 25 Caucasians. Four were from West Wateree:

      Ben D. Abbott, Harmony Baptist Church
      Mendel L. Gladden, Pine Grove Baptist Church
      James Bailey, Smyrna Methodist Church
      Moses Shannon, St. Matthew Baptist Church

The November 11, 1918 Armistice meant the returning of the troops. By April, M Company of the Kershaw County National Guard was home. The Wateree Bridge was not yet completed, and there were long lines of cars fuming to "get to the other side".

PORTRAIT PROFILE

The son of
James Abney Grigsby
and Charlotte Ann B. Reeves
The husband of
Lillian Maud Burns Grigsby Taylor
9/26/1888 - 10/30/1958

>Born in Kershaw County.
>Attended Blaney Schools, graduated from Leesville College.
>Medical Degree from Medical College of Charleston.
>1906-1948 - Blaney, S.C. Physician.
>1933-1938 - Served on the Blaney Town Council.

DR. WILLIAM DUNCAN GRIGSBY
3/21/1878 - 9/28/1948

William D. Grigsby's calling in life was being a country doctor, and he was a very good doctor and a blessing to the people of Blaney whom he served for 42 years. He delivered babies at home, made house calls for medical emergencies, too many to count, and was paid in chickens, eggs, garden vegetables, animals, and "you name it", and that was just fine with him.

In the early 1900s he built a nice house on "Blackjack Street" in town which had a waiting room for patients and a doctor's office and a medicine room with a sink where he compounded medicine for his patients. There was a little house in the backyard for the maid who helped the doctor and his wife. Also in the backyard was an open well for water. After Dr. Grigsby died he was buried in Elmwood Memorial Gardens in Columbia. Mrs. Grigsby sold the house to Ira Otis and Liddie Perry Goff who raised their family there. The house is still on the corner of what is now Church Street.

Wateree River Dam
Completed September 14,1919

The present joys of life
We doubly taste
By looking back
With pleasure on the Past...
--ANON

The Call of the Wild

Did the 20s come "roaring in", as they say, or did the 20s just blind us to the subtle changes in our lives? What happened?

The black and white equation was made more stark after the war when African American veterans returned to the "same ole, same ole", still wrapped in a blanket of "voiceless" community service. They had answered the call of the country but did not return to a welcoming community embrace. Industrial and mechanical revolution was beginning to break the surface, and agriculture was taking a back seat.

The 18th Amendment to the Constitution took effect in 1920 - National Prohibition banned the sale and manufacture of intoxicating liquors.

The 19th Amendment gave voting rights to American women. This change reached every voting precinct in Kershaw County, including Blaney. Since Reconstruction, political power had been firmly controlled by Democrats in the hands of white men. In the first week more than 60 Kershaw County women registered to vote. Still women did not immediately mount the speaking platforms at political gatherings; they continued to be "the power behind the throne", so to speak. It would be another 10 years before a woman was elected to public office.

Wartime jobs, in many cases, came to an end. The Wateree Bridge and Wateree Dam projects were over, and large numbers of laborers were unemployed. But soon the unemployed would find work in the various road improvement projects such as the 1926 paving of the Camden-to-Columbia road linking the first continuous hard surface between the two cities. The year 1927 brought the paving of the Camden-to-Charlotte road to connect three cities. In 1929, a more than two million-dollar project was announced for Federal Route No. 1 (U.S. Highway 1) to be built through Camden.

In July 1920, the boll weevil struck Kershaw County and spread like wildfire to nearly every cotton field in the county. Soon all of South Carolina was infested. In the fall cotton yields were severely reduced, textile mill orders were cut in half and they had to lay off workers. Prices were low, around 15 cents per lb., which meant that around 70% of the crop would have to pay for fertilizer, picking and ginning. In other words, it was a disaster.

Despite Governor Robert Archer Cooper's September 20 "Cotton Day" statewide meeting of farmers, improvements would not come easily. A West Wateree correspondent reported, "The boll weevil has nipped some of our prospects to make a flourishing little town out of Blaney; we feel that it will take several years for our farmers to adapt themselves to new modes of living and a more diversified crop adjustment."

The "several years" prediction took a lot longer. The year 1921 saw a yet even smaller yield due to reduced farming of cotton and the boll weevil. The next year saw Blaney farmers going to "crisis" meetings and marketing their cotton in Columbia and Camden first, then anywhere they could get a decent price. Then 1923 saw a slowdown in cotton sales, but a slight increase in business prospects. Calvin Coolidge was elected President of the United States, and a new kind of prosperity raised its head. Thirty percent of the country had electricity, and that would rise to sixty percent by the end of the decade, some said. Two hundred refrigerator models were introduced to the American public along with clothes washing machines and radios. Calvin Coolidge, in 1925, was the first President to be inaugurated with the country listening by radio. But that year the long sizzling hot summer drought and the cotton situation was so bad that farmers began to abandon boll weevil infested fields.

In 1929 cotton farmers faced the heaviest boll weevil infestation ever seen. Liberal treatments of arsenic mixed with molasses applied directly to the cotton plants, handpicking weevils and burning infected foliage seemed only to add insult to injury because nothing worked. It was all an exercise in "futility". Timber replaced cotton as a revenue source after the boll weevils got through in Blaney.

THE 1920 CENSUS - TOWN OF BLANEY
54 Families   254 People (Including children)

Occupations

22 Farmers	**2 Doctors**
6 Merchants	**1 Blacksmith**
4 Wagon Drivers	**1 Pharmacist**
3 Carpenters	**1 Horse Trader**
2 Woodcutters	**1 Railroad Section Foreman**
2 Preachers	**1 Postmaster**
2 Railroad Laborers	**1 Mail Carrier**
	1 Barber

In the 1920s up to the 1930s, Blaney was still a small farming community, but Main Street in Blaney (now Church Street) was doing a thriving business. They had a Hardware Store, Café, Shoe Shop, Grocery Stores, Dry Goods Stores, Barber Shop, Fertilizer, Feed & Seed Store, a Post Office, Doctors, Drug Store, and a 5 & 10 Cent Store. Hitching posts for horses and mule and wagons were important, for this was the mode of transportation in these Sand Hills. The town had two blacksmiths, George Glover in town and Mazzie Perry's shops on Blaney Rd and behind Henry Ross's store near Church St. Two local water mills ground corn for meal and grits - Bookman's Mill, on what is now Cherokee Ave., and Nelson's (Cureton's) Mill, now on Wildwood Lane. The town was pretty quiet during the week days as most people in the community came to town only on Saturdays for supplies.

The Vision of Henry Ford…..

The thing that was the most exciting about the 1920s was the automobile. And the man who "invented" the automobile was Henry Ford. His mechanical genius and hard-work philosophy changed the country and ushered in the 20th century consumer world.

He introduced the Model T automobile in October 1908. It was a very economical car costing $850, 4 cylinder, 1200 lbs., 40MPH, durable, simple to repair, green color at first, then black. Farmers, doctors, salesmen, merchants, just "everybody" bought this car. It brought joy and freedom to people's lives. The Blaney community felt "lifted out of the sand".

The market was immense and so successful that in 1910 Ford built a new factory and was turning out 1000 of the Model T every day. By 1913 he controlled the American car market. He achieved his goals through adopting a new thing - an assembly line. In 1914 Ford Motor Co. had a profit of $26 million. He paid the assembly line workers $5.00 per day and reduced their hours of labor from 9 to 8. By doing this he solved his turnover problem caused by the repetitive, monotonous, boring assembly line work. No wonder 10,000 men wanted to work at his plant.

In 1920 a great variety of models and prices of automobiles was on the market. Not just Fords anymore but Chevrolets, Oldsmobile's, and Buicks were available. Even though the roads around Blaney were still mostly sand and clay, automobiles began to appear more and more in the community. Advertisements for the period touted the many garages selling gas and servicing the autos (breakdowns and accidents were frequent), and the public was reminded to buy automobile insurance. W. T. Redfern was the local Ford dealer in Camden and displayed all the stylish new Ford models, for Ford Motor Co. was stopping its 18 year production of the standard, popular, economical Model T. New pleasure cars were selling for $385 to $570 and trucks for $460 to $610. On May 26, 1927, the last Model T rolled off the assembly line - the 15 millionth.

South Carolina would issue the first drivers licenses in 1930 while the first drivers license examinations would not start until 1933.

But don't cry for Henry Ford. In December 1927 he introduced a new model, the Model A, which would be available on the installment plan. He sold 700,000 the first year. In 1928 he built a huge new plant with 93 buildings which could produce 10,000 cars a day. It employed 75,000 people working around the clock in shifts.

The 1929 stock market crash caused consumerism to bottom out. Model A sales fell off, and there was a big employee lay-off at the Ford plant. To top it all, union organizers came (UAW), and Ford had to turn the company over to his son, Edsel.

But the genius of Henry Ford lives on as I think we will all agree.

Quenching the Thirst...

Would you have guessed that some folks stockpiled beverage alcohol after the 18th Prohibition Amendment was enacted and before the amendment took effect? They did, indeed, and were able to ride out the "dry" 13 years (1920-1933) of the ban on the sale of liquor everywhere in the U. S. Others could turn to "moonshine" or "bootlegging" to get their thirst satisfied. Illegal activities, including many stills, were rampant during prohibition, and police activity was "very active."

The 1923 visit to Camden by the well known evangelist, Billy Sunday, drew large crowds to Camden Baptist Church. He was an ardent supporter of Prohibition and spoke frankly about the need for salvation and social reform. His words made an impact on the congregations, and many came forward to pray. Many in the crowd were from Blaney, Bethune, and Bishopville.

Under-funded and under-manned law enforcement worked hard to abate the ever-flowing "strong drink," but with hidden stills operating from Kershaw County swamps, officers had to rely on local tips or observations to curb the activity. They learned to watch for drunken insects flying over the fermenting mash or animals staggering along the river roads. Most of the stills were in West Wateree where officers at certain times found nearly a still a day as reported by the April 8, 1927 *Camden Chronicle*.

First Woman Elected…

In November 1920, compulsory education for children began in Kershaw County. However, it was not enforced because the county lacked a truant officer. In 1919 there was only one white high school in the county (Camden), but by 1929 there were seven, including Blaney. There remained only one black high school in the county, Jackson in Camden.

In 1929 the first woman was elected to a public office in Kershaw County. Kathleen B. Watts was elected as the Superintendent of Education, a 4-year term. She had been principal of Lugoff School and head of Antioch High School. She really pushed parent-teacher communication and cooperation so that students could learn in the best environment possible. Also in 1929 Herbert Hoover was elected President of the United States. He was a Quaker and humanitarian and promised the people "a chicken in every pot and a car in every garage."

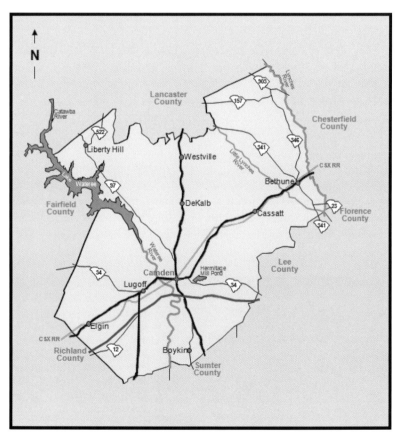

2008 Map of Kershaw County

PORTRAIT PROFILE

The daughter of
Lewis Lee Young and Ollie Truesdale

The wife of James Henry Koon

STEP-CHILDREN
Juanita Koon Aldrich 6/24/1929
Sarah Koon McKenzie 12/2/1930 - 2003

SALLY YOUNG KOON
8/19/1902 - 9/1/1968

>Taught public elementary school for 40+ years.
> Graduated from Newberry & Winthrop College in Rock Hill, S.C.
> Member of Union Baptist Church, Elgin,S.C. and is buried there.

Sally Koon was born in the Flat Rock area of Kershaw County. She taught school first at the age of 18 in the Pontiac area of Richland County. In 1938 she taught seven grades at Crescent School, a one-room school located on Kennedy Road at Goff Circle which is south of interstate I20. It still stands as a part of the Woodrow Goff residence. The majority of her teaching career was teaching the third grade to Blaney students in Blaney, S. C. She was a well-respected, "no-nonsense" teacher who taught her students what they needed to be a success in life.

Third grade class from 1944 taught by Mrs. Sally Koon

Starting far left 1st row, Margie R. Crowley, Ann Zorn, Hammy Moak, Ida Mae J. Anderson, boy unknown, boy unknown, Mae McKay, boy unknown and Leo Ross. 2nd row far left, Ruby M. Jeffers, Sivas Ross, Dorothy Branham, Wylean Goff, girl unknown, Mary Lois McPherson, Tommy Kirkland, Bobby E. Goff, boy unknown, boy unknown, boy unknown. 3rd row far left, Ray Miles, boy unknown, Erine Moak, girl unknown, boy unknown, girl unknown, Arlin Kirkland, girl unknown, girl unknown, Ivy Kelly and boy unknown.

 IX

Never Give Up! If adversity presses,
Providence wisely has mingled the cup,
And the best counsel, in all your distresses,
Is the stout watchword of
Never Give Up!
--Martin F. Tupper

Bread Cast Upon the Waters

The 1929 stock market crash added to the wettest year on record locally with three tornadoes thrown in for good measure. But that paled beside the new decade of super high summer temperatures with drought, crop failures, lack of money, and no hope that things would get any better.

THE 1930 CENSUS OF THE TOWN OF BLANEY
44 Families   175 People (Including children)
Occupations

8 Farmers	1 School Supt.
2 Merchants	3 Teachers
3 Sales Clerks	1 Railroad Agent
1 Blacksmith	1 Cotton Mill Worker
1 Physician	1 Railroad Section Foreman
1 Postmaster	2 Truck Drivers
1 Mail Carrier	1 Barber
1 Construction Foreman	1 Night watchman
1 Auto Mechanic	1 Laundress
1 Telegraph Operator	11 Laborers

Blaney citizens felt that things could not get worse, but as the hard times continued and local attempts to deal with the suffering brought little relief, they began to think only federal money could solve some of the more serious unemployment problems. President Herbert Hoover finally set up a public works project just before he left office. Blaney citizens along with the rest of the country were relieved and encouraged by the inauguration of President Franklin D. Roosevelt who addressed the "Great Depression" immediately with promises of a "New Deal" of change for the better. After years of despair, Roosevelt's speeches lifted the nation. He spoke to America by radio weekly in what were called "Fireside Chats."

Banks began to close locally, and business failures were common as the financial crisis tightened. Railroads were in trouble, even the Seaboard Railroad faced receivership. With 12% unemployment, county residents searched for jobs far afield, leaving families behind to fend for themselves. South Carolina could not pay schoolteachers, and it was feared the schools would not reopen when scheduled. Many children lacking clothes and books could not return to school. Some had to stay out to help families as farm laborers. The children who did attend school rose at daylight to complete family farm chores before going to school. Though cars were not in abundance on the roads around Blaney, on October 1, 1930, the law required a driving test and a 50 cent fee for a license to drive. Old licenses were grandfathered provided the driver was over twelve years of age.

County fairs organized by county agents in 1930 encouraged communities to "put your best foot forward" in handiwork, arts, canning, farm products, and baked goods. The exhibits were judged, and ribbons were given for prizes. There were fairs at Blaney, Bethune, Antioch, Cassatt, Charlotte Thompson, Liberty Hill, Mt. Pisgah, and Pine Grove with a Clemson judge at each. The Blaney fair was "standing room only" and had more exhibits than expected. Blaney displayed more than 15 kinds of fresh vegetables, canned fruits, needlework, and flowers. An afternoon of fun and games boosted the spirits of all in attendance.

The 1932 Blaney Community Fair presented cut flowers and potted plants for judging as well as 25 varieties of fresh vegetables, jellies, pickles, cakes, breads, and needlework. Special attention was paid to J. M. Martin's ribbon cane and sorghum and to the huge pumpkin entered by H. A. Hawkins.

1931 saw the completion of the midpoint of U.S. Highway #1 near Cheraw about 60 miles from Camden. The first national highway now ran in a continuous hard surface from Canada to Miami, linking all state capitols along the way. It followed the old Sand Hills route, crossing and re-crossing the Seaboard Railway through Kershaw County. It threaded through Blaney's Main Street intersection southward to our state capitol in Columbia. Before the paved road, the trip to Columbia on dirt roads took all day. A trip by mule and wagon would take two days. It was a motor car operator's dream and a boon for merchants in Blaney who would benefit from the road traffic at their front doors.

The 1932 charity in the form of flour donated by the federal government for distribution by the Red Cross was at first a pleasant surprise but turned into frustration by the "red tape" that slowed the much needed commodity from getting into the hands of those who needed it most. First, a written application and an endorsement verifying the need had to be approved, then an appearance in person to pick up the flour at the distribution point was required. Problems included pride, incomplete paperwork, and lack of transportation. Six Hundred barrels for a three month supply came by railway boxcars. There were 4800 sacks of flour distributed to Kershaw County's needy residents. Blaney residents received fatback, beans, syrup, grits, and meal to go with the flour. All of the food came by railroad. The federal government also donated 13,500 yards of cotton fabric with the stipulation that the cloth must be made into garments before distribution. Not to be outdone, local volunteers went to work cutting and sewing 4500 garments which really was helpful to a large number of county people.

Dr. William D. Grigsby, the only Blaney physician, was extremely busy trying to take care of people in the Blaney community who were malnourished due to poor diets, especially in those who were unemployed. Common illnesses abounded caused by bad sanitation, no window screens, and impure drinking water from open wells or springs, because a lot of people just could not afford to do better. Warren Sanders provided the town with running water, but water was scarce, and the small wells, 2" in diameter with an old pump that pumped only half the time with a 6" stroke and 5-6 gal. minimum, made water service difficult. Mr. E. T. Bowen had four wells for his Blaney Lumber Co. and also furnished water for a good many families. After that, Mr. Mosby Perry began putting down pumps, and Mr. Ira Goff was the community well digger. Dr. A. W. Humphries, County Health Director, believed education about better food choices would improve the situation, but the climbing poverty rate prevented the message from getting to the people who simply did not have enough to eat, nor money to buy the right kind of food.

Camden Hospital was treating a large number of charity patients, and fund raisers in all communities were started to meet the hospital crisis. Thanksgiving was set aside as "Pounding Day for the Hospital", and farmers donated produce instead of cash to the fund drive.

When Prohibition was repealed in 1933, taverns with beer on tap became the rage, and coffee shops replaced traditional tea rooms. The Broad Street Lunch opened across from the Kershaw County Courthouse serving a beef patty on hand sliced loaf bread, "the first hamburger" for many. In Lugoff, Gus Ward opened a restaurant on (Hwy. #1) Camden-Columbia Highway and served meals featuring beef and barbeque.

High School football lifted spirits and excited fans as schools began competitions avidly followed. Cockfighting, though illegal, had a big following with one contest in Camden featuring 20 towns from three states entering combatants. But the most popular entertainment was - Radio. While radio had been around in the 20s, by the end of the 30s, despite hard times, everybody had a radio. And most people listened to WIS radio stationed in Columbia. W-I-S were the call letters for "Wonderful Iodine State," a South Carolina slogan of the 30s. Most people did not have electricity but received broadcasts by antennae attached to quartz crystal sets. Families would gather around these bulky static-prone machines at night to listen to sounds of all kinds of news reports, music, comedy, and drama like *Amos and Andy*, the *Lux Radio Theater*, and, *The Lone Ranger* with Tonto, or talks of every description. Young adults loved going to the Majestic Theater owned by T. Lee Little in Camden to see and hear the latest innovation, a sound system with pictures - moving pictures. The old silent films were no longer in vogue.

In hard times, many people turned to their faith, and religious preaching gave great solace. Revivals would go on for a long time, even weeks in some cases as people prayed, wept, shouted, praised and "spoke in tongues". Worshippers sought relief through the singing of the hymns of the faith and personal contact with like sufferers. Two remaining campgrounds at Blaney and Bethune speak to us of those by-gone days when "big meetings" gave "big blessings".

Willie S. Cormer Revival promotion
Courtesy of the Blaney-Elgin Museum & Historical Society

Adolph Hitler became Chancellor of Germany in January 1933, and as the Nazi regime grew, many pulpits in churches in the county presented messages to compare contemporary times with biblical prophesies of the future. Rev. Willie S. Cromer, who was Pastor of Blaney Baptist Church at the time, was a strong biblical preacher who reminded his charges of the awesome power of the Word in understanding world events. He also served as Pastor of Union Baptist Church from 1933 to 1936, and Sandhill Heights Baptist Church in the 70s. He is remembered in the Blaney community as not only a man of God but a shepherd to the people.

The recently built airport at Camden did not attract the average Blaney man's attention, but more and more as he stood in an isolated cotton field, he would catch sight of a small airplane making its way across the sky. He had a home without electricity, no indoor plumbing, and no telephone - and yet he was stirred by this visible dot in the sky and its potential for changes that would make his life better. In 1932, aviation caught the average man's attention when Camden was added to the U. S. Postal Service's airmail route contracted with Eastern Airways.

The celebrated rigid dirigible, Akron, circled low over Kershaw County early one morning. Built by Goodyear at 782 feet long, buoyed by nonflammable helium and powered by 8 engines, the giant military airship could launch and retrieve five airplanes in flight. The *Camden Chronicle* reported, "Lights were burning on the vessel and many were thrilled at the sight of the big air traveler." Two years later the dirigible crashed at sea killing most of the crew.

The New Deal...

Newly elected President Franklin D. Roosevelt called Congress into a special 100 day session in March 1933. Every program he requested of the Congress was enacted, a record amount of major legislation in such a short period of time. These three actions were of special note:

1. The 21st Amendment to the Constitution was ratified ending Prohibition.
2. Taxes were levied on newly legalized alcohol sales.
3. On March 6 all the nation's banks closed to audit books and only sound banks reopened. New deposits were secured by Federal insurance.
   >First National Bank in Camden reopened without restriction.
   >Bank of Camden remained closed to reorganize into The Commercial Bank of Camden.
   >First Savings and Loan opened in 1934.

Will Rogers, the noted humorist remarked, "Folks said if Roosevelt had burned down the White House, at least he got a fire going."

The most popular New Deal program proved to be the CCC (Civilian Conservation Corps). In addition to its original mission to serve national forests, it added state forest and private land programs for states like South Carolina that had no national forests. Employment relief was offered to single young men 18-25 for six months.

They were paid $30 a month of which $25 was sent directly to their families. The impact on relief families was astonishing, and the areas near the camps benefited not only from the workers labor and camp related spending but families now had cash to spend.

The county's first CCC camp was established about three miles north of Blaney near Hood's Pond area, and about two miles from U. S. Hwy. #1.

An old 800-acre estate called Wildwood Manor was made available by Karl T. Roseborough of Lugoff, and in July 1933, they erected a dining hall, tents, recreation building, telephone pole, electric lines, dug a well, and installed a water tank. It was notable that this was the only place in the county with rural electric service and a telephone. Of course they put up a flag pole with the American flag flying, and they had a radio so they could listen directly to President Roosevelt and his cabinet members.

The Blaney community lost no time making the camp personnel welcome. A "Homecoming Week" was celebrated in August at the camp and in Camden. Guitarist Monroe Tucker, a CCC camper, wrote a song about the rain and windstorm in Blaney the night of the homecoming celebration. "Falling Tents" was published in the *Camden Chronicle*. The surrounding churches saw a number of campers in church on the Sundays they were encamped.

The camp was named "The Richmond Hobson Hilton Camp" in honor of a Kershaw County war hero who drowned in Lake Murray trying to save boating accident victims. On August 25 at Blaney a ceremony unveiled a memorial tablet to Hilton (This tablet is preserved in the Memorial Room of American Legion Post 17 in Camden). This was followed with a barbecue in the camp's recreation center named Guion Hall for West Wateree's Louie I. Guion, a state forestry leader.

The work done in the county by these men was not only very labor intensive but heart-warming to witness. They cleaned up eroded and used-up land, dug ditches for drainage where needed, built roads, planted trees, put in fire breaks, and even fought woods fires. Everyone was sorry to see the camp close and the workers move on to help establish Manchester State Forest in Sumter County.

But Camp Hilton "rose again" when a work camp called S.C. Veterans Camp No. 4 moved in using war veterans regardless of age or marital status to continue the projects started by the first encampment. Reporting for duty in August 1935, were 265 veterans. Disaster struck in the form of a hurricane which devastated the Florida Keys where 259 veterans lost their lives at a Florida Veterans Camp. The federal administration in the face of criticism for not protecting the veterans enough, moved immediately to close the South Carolina veterans camps. The men were either enrolled in other CCC camps, sent home, or dispersed to other camps. The *Camden Chronicle* for September 27, 1935, reported that 104 of the men at the Blaney camp had signed with the CCC.

Mention should be made of the CCC labor which helped complete a telephone-linked system of steel fire towers, firebreaks, and roads for firefighting. The third fire tower was constructed at Blaney in 1933 and was linked to Camden and Liberty Hill towers, and in 1936 two more towers were erected in Westville and Cassatt. In 1946 the Buffalo fire tower completed the last of six towers covering the entire county. At first wardens served as tower keepers, reporting fires and then joining ground crews to fight fires. The hiring of separate tower keepers came later.

Another big government program begun in 1935 would make a huge impact on the nation's people for years to come - Social Security. Cards with Social Security numbers would be issued to every American from birth and be a defining number for identification and many other uses in every citizen's lifetime.

President Franklin Roosevelt traveled by train as his preferred mode of travel and actually stopped in Blaney in the mid-thirties to greet the citizens. It was a great occasion, and hundreds of people showed up at the Railroad Depot to see him and wish him "God-speed". The school children got out of school to see him and made a big "commotion" which cheered everyone. The farmers were there in big numbers because they had been the recipients of seed loans established by President Roosevelt and Congress to help them buy fertilizer and seed to farm with during the depression.

A Bridge Over Troubled Waters…

As more and more automobiles traveled U. S. Highway #1, more and more drivers of those automobiles were doing a slow burn every time they had to cross the toll bridge over the Wateree River. Blaney folks went to Camden and back to Blaney many times in a week to transact business, go to doctors, shop, or just to visit, and every time they had to pay a toll to use the bridge. Many complained that since the highway was built with federal money they should not have to pay another tax to use the bridge. Officials reminded them that the bridge was built with county money which they borrowed, and the toll on the bridge was necessary to pay off the loan on the bridge, not the road. This was just too complicated for most people to understand, so they continued to complain. An appeal was made to the legislature to solve the problem.

The State General Assembly agreed to buy the Wateree Bridge and paid Kershaw County $147,500. They rushed to take down the hated toll house on the bridge and resurfaced the road. But best of all, the toll stopped on April 30, 1934.

But the bridge story doesn't stop there. There was a bad accident on the bridge in April 1938 involving a two ton truck that skidded off the icy bridge and plunged into the waters below. The fuel tanks exploded and burned seven spans of the old wooden bridge. Repairs were made and the bridge was passable again in just a few days. but all the traffic had been rerouted miles and miles out into the county in order to cross the river. Officials realized that a longer detour of traffic would not only enrage the travelers but severely hamper the county economy. So off to the drawing board for a plan for a new, stronger, straight bridge to be built about 2000 feet downstream from the old wooden bridge which would remain in use until the new bridge was finished.

Works Progress Administration…

The WPA was part of the "New Deal" government projects in President Roosevelt's plan to provide employment while improving communities.

Blaney High School got a badly needed auditorium, and frame schoolhouses with 2-8 rooms were constructed in 1938 by the WPA in the community. The auditorium had theater type seating for about 350 people, a stage with large curtains, and a brand new piano. It was used for school assemblies, plays, graduations, piano recitals, and a host of other events the community could attend and enjoy. It was also used a few times for weddings. (In 1937 by state law, females could marry at the age of 14 with parental consent or age 18 without consent. Males under 21 had to have parental consent to marry.) The auditorium was well used and was the pride and joy of Blaney.

Blaney Ordinances...

Intendent (Mayor) Samuel Walter Rose, along with Wardens Jack G. Ross, William D. Grigsby, J. Paul Ross and Earl Talmadge Bowen, enacted some town ordinances in 1938 that were recorded by the Town Clerk, Mary Rabon.

>>Prohibit sale, transport, and storing of intoxicating beverages and
   liquors and sale of liquid flavoring extracts with excess of 1%
   alcohol or ether.
>>Regulate drivers of motor vehicles under the influence of whiskey,
   reckless driving, fixing speed limits, and parking within the town
   providing for penalties for violation.
>>Forbidding disorderly conduct, cruising, fighting, or affray and
   indecent exposure.
>>Prohibit the carrying of concealed weapons.
>>Raise supplies for the town for the year 1938.
>>Require payment of license tax on business, occupation, or profession
   for 1938.

1938 Ordinance for Business License Fees:
Class #2 (Gross Annual Income $1000 or less)
(Over $1000 will be 10 cents per $1000)

Railway Express Co.	$ 5.00	Trucks delivering goods & such	10.00
Meat Markets/Green Grocers	10.00	as gasoline, drinks, tobacco,	
Horse, Cow or Livestock Dealer	10.00	candy, drugs, bread, peanuts,	
Lawyer, Physician, Dentist	10.00	fruits, etc.	
Blacksmith Shop per Forge	5.00	Garage with auto accessories	15.00
Barber Shop per Chair	2.00	& filling station	
Fertilizer & Cotton seed Dealer	10.00	Filling Station alone & not	10.00
Cross tie, Lumber/Timber Dealer	10.00	attached to Gen. Mdse.	
Shows, according to size per Day	2.00 to 10.00	Saw Mills	10.00
		Planing Mills	15.00
		Ginnings (cotton gins) up to 300 saws	10.00

Section 5	From $	To $	Fee $
Merchants			
Annual Sales	1.00	10,000	10.00
	10,000	20,000	15.00
	20,000	30,000	20.00
	30,000	50,000	25.00
	50,000	75,000	30.00
	75,000	100,000	40.00
	100,000+	above	50.00

Fred Hunter and Afon Strickland at Blaney Lumber Mill -1950.
Courtesy of Van Strickland

Electricity came to the town of Blaney in 1927. A 22,000 volt rural line was pulled by Carolina Power & Light Co. from Camden to Lugoff to Blaney. Until that time Blaney had used large lanterns and gas lights for study and daily living needs. Fireplaces were the only heat. Rural areas would have to wait until the 40s for electricity. Trains were still used by many people. The train for Columbia would come through about 11:00 AM going south and return from Columbia to Blaney going north around 4:00 PM. Trip cost was 25 cents each way. The only telephone in town was in Henry Ross's Grocery Store. The S. Henry Ross family operated 4-5 grocery stores in the county and had large warehouses in Blaney to service the stores.

Sounds of War…

If you were alert and listened carefully, you could hear the drumbeat, the unmistakable sword rattling portrayed in the local news and on the radio. Hitler and Mussolini were names heard again and again in connection with military events a world away in 1937. We were distracted for a time with the disappearance and search for Amelia Earhart, the beloved aviatrix who was trying to fly around the world but mysteriously disappeared over the ocean somewhere in the Pacific.

In 1939 Britain and France declared war on Germany, and blood pressures went up in America's people, young and old, for they knew the die was cast.

PORTRAIT PROFILE

EARL TALMADGE BOWEN
11/22/1897 - 9/25/1976

The son of
Earl Bowen and Annie L. Bowen
The husband of
Sally P. Bowen and Jean S. Bowen

CHILDREN (Sally)
Sarah Bowen Emanuel
GRANDCHILDREN
B.J., Cammy, Rebecca and Sally

E. T. Bowen wore many hats, but, dating from 1943, when he executed his first soil and water conservation plan, farming was his main vocation. By 1957, when he was selected as the Outstanding Conservation Farmer in Kershaw County, he had 250 acres of cotton and 60 acres of corn and cover crops on 17 farms including his homeplace farm which had been in the Bowen Family for five generations. He had 10 irrigation ponds on the homeplace with grass planted in 35 acres of waterways and seven miles of terraces for 100 acres of cotton. He had 75 acres of Coastal Bermuda and 500 acres of trees. He said he believed that conservation farming would mean the most for the future-- future for his four granddaughters.

In 1957, Mr. Bowen had been in business for 35 years establishing the Blaney Lumber Co., Planing Mill, Warehouses, Sawmill, Hardware Store, Blaney Drug Store, Farmers Supply, cotton gin, and others. He was a cotton broker and had extensive land and timber holdings in Kershaw, Richland, and Fairfield counties. He served on the Blaney Town Council in 1933, 1938, and 1954 and on many county boards and committees including the Camden Hospital Board. He was a member of Salem United Methodist Church in Elgin, S. C., where he is buried.

Bowen Home

The Flag - The Star - The Window

The Boy Scout motto is "Be Prepared", and most Americans in 1939 took that advice seriously. They knew the government headed by President Roosevelt, now in his second term, took it seriously when Camp Jackson was activated and renamed Fort Jackson. They spent millions for expansion of the fort and condemned enough land around the fort to double its area to 53,000 acres. Something was definitely going to happen; it was just a question of when, exactly. All the surrounding communities, including Blaney, benefited from the expansion.

The first peace-time conscription of eligible men happened in 1940. Draft registration day was October 16, and the registration took place in the local schools by the school teachers. The day was declared a state holiday as Kershaw County registered 3375 men, ages 21-35. A lottery selected the men actually drafted for a one year tour of duty. Blue flags with a white star began to go up in front windows of the homes where servicemen had been called up for duty.

Call-ups in the prewar buildup touched many families in the county including the South Carolina National Guard Unit, Company M, 118th Infantry composed of "crackerjack" men ordered to Fort Jackson for a year of active duty. The "Carolina Maneuvers" in 1941 were nine months in preparation for two months of winter war games designed to test equipment and game plans for defending against tanks in combat. The games were purposefully scheduled for the months of October and November because crop gathering would be over and quail hunting was cancelled in 14 counties including Kershaw. These maneuvers, conducted all over the county, were headquartered in Camden and featured the notorious Gen. George S. Patton, whose active involvement garnered public support for rearmament.

The Blaney area and U. S. Highway #1 lay between the two "warring" armies (Ft. Bragg and Ft. Jackson) that would battle in 80,000 acres in the county. The entire mock battle area covered over 10,000 square miles in North and South Carolina. The county maneuvers director was Ernest C. Zemp of Camden who was appointed by Governor Burnet R. Maybank. The publicity both for the state and local communities like Blaney was priceless, and the 67 million spent by the military fueled a recharged economy in the county.

One of the long term benefits of the maneuvers was the 1941 construction of a safer Wateree Bridge brought about after an army truck and a log truck sideswiped the bridge structure, and bridge load limits were set and enforced while repairs were made. The resulting traffic snarls and reports from the two-state maneuvers area of the deaths of 93 soldiers (due in large part to unrelated motor vehicle accidents) during the two month maneuvers propelled the government realization that a new and safer Wateree Bridge on U.S. Highway #1 was important for national security as well as daily local travel and emergency use. The new modern concrete and steel bridge was completed in 1942, widened in 1968, and renamed the Howard F. Speaks Bridge.

"Meanwhile back at the ranch", so to speak, locals were still farming with mules rather than tractors, and agricultural items were still for sale at S. Henry Ross's store (he also sold coffins or caskets in a side building) and Jack Bailey's Milling Distribution Co. in Blaney. Fertilizer, potash, seeds, and feeds continued to be best sellers. Farmers were still raising hogs, cattle, and (the 3 p's) peas, potatoes, and peanuts. Ads in newspapers had "help wanted" for tenant farmers and share-cropping farmers. In 1941 cotton farmers had the smallest crop since Reconstruction due to---you guessed it---the boll weevil. The government recommended planting kudzu to enrich eroded soils and was even willing to pay farmers for converting to these soil protecting crops. It was thought by some that one of the causes of soil infertility was the build-up of arsenic in fields that were repeatedly dusted in earlier years. Arsenic buildup in clay soil affected crops more than in sandy soil.

Rural Electrification…

If I had to tell you what I think was the most beneficial government program during President Roosevelt's tenure, it would be the Rural Electrification Program. In rural Blaney community in 1941 the project began connecting electricity to individual homes. There was no more studying for school by kerosene lamps, no more ironing with an "iron" iron heated on the laundry heater, no more dressing in the dark to go to work and school, no more cooking on a wood stove, and no more buying real ice for the "Ice Box." Carrying water to the house from the well was history. It made the difference of a life time. Of course, it took until the end of the 1940s to finish getting power in the Blaney area, but rural homeowners highly rated this program above all others.

There was a struggle in the early 40s to attract enough physicians to the county to treat the normal sick patient population. It was a matter of real concern, especially to county health officials, that there just might be a disaster in the making in case an epidemic of some disease reared its ugly head. Just such a panic ensued when, in early 1941, a flu epidemic exploded. Community gatherings were cancelled, and a number of schools were closed. Blaney schools in January, along with most of West Wateree schools, Kershaw City schools, and Bethune schools in February closed, causing an overflow of hospital patients in Camden Hospital. But the leading concern was tuberculosis, and Kershaw County had no treatment facilities, no preventive vaccine, and no known drug cure. There were 22 patients placed in the state sanatorium for treatment in 1940, and five patients died in December 1940 in the county. Out of the 1000 teachers and school children tested for TB in 1941 in the county, 20% were found positive to the living TB germs. The Tuberculosis Association launched an educational program to teach the public the characteristics of the disease and its deadly effects.

A Date Which Will Live In Infamy…

Everybody who was alive on Sunday, December 7, 1941 can remember what they were doing when they heard over the radio about the attack on Pearl Harbor by the Japanese. It was so shocking and frightening that the event was placed in our memory banks forever.

President Roosevelt in his 3ʳᵈ term of office had become a "Father Figure" to America since he had regularly visited families by radio, establishing an emotional bond, and he had America's undivided attention when he delivered a live radio presidential address to a Joint Session of Congress on December 8, 1941, the day after the Japanese attack. He reassured the nation that even though the "dastardly" attack had caused many American lives to be lost, he had "directed that all measures be taken for our defense." The first line of the seven-minute speech described the previous day as, "a date which will live in infamy", and he urged the American people to never forget the attack, and memorialize its date. Within an hour of the speech, Congress passed a formal declaration of war against Japan and officially brought the United States into World War II.

Mr. Bickley, Superintendent of Blaney Schools called all students and teachers into the Blaney School Auditorium on Monday, December 8, 1941, (after roll call and morning devotional using the Bible which had been approved for use in school) to hear Roosevelt declare war on Japan via radio. Everyone was crying and emotionally upset, so school was dismissed for the day.

The county responded with a surge of men volunteering for military duty and reporting within days of the attack. Blaney sweethearts exchanged wedding vows before the men had to leave for training in a number of cases, and citizens one and all searched for something, anything, that would be helpful in the war effort. Many volunteered for civil defense responsibilities cooperating in doing what was necessary to protect their communities.

The Blaney community contributed a great many things needed for the war effort. A call for more pulpwood sent workers into the forests to cut timber that would be used to make everything from explosives to parachutes. Jack Bailey, Charlie Wooten and E. Talmadge Bowen were at the forefront of the push and worked their crews overtime to meet the war-time needs. Drives for waste paper, rubber and scrap metal (iron, steel, copper, and brass) went into overdrive with the Blaney schoolchildren collecting 5,552 lbs. of waste paper in 1942. Anderson Goff bought iron and steel for 1 cent/ lb., and Jack Bailey bought copper and brass for 25 cents/ lb. Mr. Skipper bought rubber. (Skipper's Auto Service in Blaney was a gasoline filling station that handled auto and truck parts, tires, batteries, electric appliances, auto repairs, and a wrecker service.)

A new federal draft law in 1942 lowered the age for call-up from 20 to 18. In April 1943 the draft age was extended from 45 to 65. Again schools were the site for registering, and school teachers did the registration. As you would expect, the town of Blaney had almost no men left to draft, and the women stepped up to the plate to keep the home fires burning.

It was at this point in the war years that more women were elected to leadership positions in the county government. Positions usually occupied by men now filled by women included Kathleen Watts, Superintendent of Education; Lena Clyburn, Clerk of Court; Maggie McLeod, Sheriff; and Etta Hough, Game Warden. No town records exist that would tell us who served as the mayor of Blaney or the council members during the war years, but it's a good bet some of them were women! Mary Rabon and Mattie Ross were the town clerks during this time and just maybe they handled the mayor's job, too!

Conserve, Recycle, Substitute, Do Without…

The first thing to be rationed was rubber goods and auto tires since the Japanese claimed most of the world's rubber trees effectively shutting down all manufacture of rubber goods. Detroit switched over to war-time production and stopped making civilian cars. So, owning your own car was a challenge especially since auto parts were scarce and gasoline was rationed, too. Car pools solved some of the problem and bicycles the rest. As the war wore on we saw sugar, meat, coffee, butter, shoes, kerosene, and coal rationed, and keeping up with ration card books and stamps was a real chore.

Jack E. Bailey was the corps commander in Blaney for the Kershaw County Council of Defense and supervised one of the county's observation posts which was on 24-hour duty. The Blaney fire tower operator spotted for airplanes, and air raid drills and blackouts were practiced in the schools and homes. Mr. Bailey devised an emergency signal which alerted the Blaney townspeople to possible enemy attacks. It went off one day and to everyone's surprise, "enemy" airplanes appeared over the town, scattering everyone back inside. It turned out it was a practice bombing attack by some Shaw field army planes. The "all-clear" signal was a big relief.

Daylight savings time began in 1942 and aided workers who needed to be home before "lights out" at night. The "blackouts" experienced in other parts of the county were not so prevalent in Blaney since rural electricity had not been hooked up in much of the community, and the town's dependence on the trains diminished since the military had priority over train travel.

On May 1, 1942, dedication of the new $350,000 Wateree Bridge featured a motorcade of county officials coming from the east meeting a similar motorcade coming from the west meeting together at a ribbon barrier as twelve large planes saluted the event overhead. Built 1000 yards south of the old wooden bridge, the straight 1950 foot bridge of reinforced concrete with a 26 ft. wide roadway and sidewalks glistened in the bright light of day as expressions of satisfaction in a job well done echoed throughout the county.

This war was "close to home" as evidenced by the empty chairs at dinner tables in the Blaney community and all over the county. By the end of 1943, twenty men had given their lives in defense of our country. In 1945 it was reported that two African American families had seen six sons go to war - Boykin and Charity Belton of Blaney and Lemuel and Fannie Belton of Camden. Everyone dreaded the sight of a boy delivering a telegram or a knock on the front door. Early in 1945 word came that Captain Arthur T. Simpson of Blaney was confirmed killed. He had previously been listed as missing in action.

German prisoners of war were being shipped to America by the hundreds in 1945 away from the fierce fighting going on in Europe

In April several hundred were assigned to Camden. Some of them ended up in Blaney working during the daytime at the Blaney Lumber Mill owned by E. Talmadge Bowen. At night they were sent back to Camden to be confined in the prisoner of war camp set up there enclosed by barbed wire. For the most part they cooperated with their captors and at the end of the war were sent back to Germany.

President Harry S. Truman had the sad duty to announce the death of President Franklin Delano Roosevelt on May 12, 1945. The nation could hardly believe it. We were still at war with Japan, and our victory over Germany celebrated on May 8 was still in the mopping up stage. How could we change leaders at this point? Just who was this Harry Truman anyway? President Roosevelt was not only our president serving in his fourth term of office, but he was like a member of the family, so it was a very personal loss as well as national. Many believe until this very day that Franklin Roosevelt was the most important leader this country has ever had.

The Japanese were still fighting when, on August 6 and 9, atomic bombs were dropped on Hiroshima and Nagasaki . In one stroke,100,000 people were disintegrated. The Japanese surrendered August 14, 1945, and at long last World War II was over.

The After Years…

Ninety-eight county soldiers were killed in World War II. A mixed blessing for their sacrifice enabled us to remain free even while individual families mourned their passing. The world would be forever changed, and the challenges began immediately.

Blacktop paving projects after the war included U. S. Highway #1 from Lugoff to Blaney and on to Columbia. It would be straightened and re-surfaced. The West Wateree Route 27 (present Hwy. 34) would be re-surfaced from Lugoff to the Fairfield County line. A new service station for automobiles opened on U.S. Highway #1 in 1948 called "Town and Country" near Camden. The ESSO station had six gasoline pumps and was open 24 hours a day, 7 days a week. It had a snack bar, clock tower and hundreds of feet of plate glass. It was a work of art to see and use. Also in 1948, the first mechanical "cotton picker" in the county could be bought at Whitaker and Co. on Rutledge St. in Camden. Blaney farmers shipped fifteen train cars of watermelons each week in July 1949. Another sign of the modern times approaching was the replacement of the Seaboard Railroad trestle over the Wateree River with new steel spans and up-to-date piers needed for the heavier and faster trains of the future.

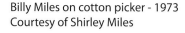
Billy Miles on cotton picker - 1973
Courtesy of Shirley Miles

The new threat of nuclear anniliation faced the world. The USA now became known as a "super power", and with that power came immense responsibility. When Winston Churchill warned in 1946 that an "iron curtain" was descending between free and communist nations, we knew that the "Cold War" had begun. The GI Bill of Rights provided returning veterans an education, job training, and housing loans, except rights for women and blacks were limited. Prices went up in 1946 as the post-war economy took off. Homes were bought along with appliances, and cars, and change was the name of the game. Kershaw County had changed drastically and would continue to do so in the immediate future. The *Camden Chronicle* reported on October 31, 1946, that the first county casualty of World War II had returned. PFC David W. Reynolds was buried at Smyrna Church in West Wateree. He was killed two years earlier on October 8, 1944, in Germany.

Blaney citizens who were appointed to important committees in 1947 included Mattie Ross to Blaney School Lunchroom Manager where children were served hot, nourishing meals that cost 15 cents. Mrs. C. R. Bowen was on the Kershaw County Library Commission and Miss Isaiah Bowen, Dr. William D. Grigsby, and Edwin L. (Shorty) Sessions were on the Kershaw County Committee to handle the funded Recreation Program for Blaney Youth. Playgrounds and sports equipment were placed in schools. Jesse T. Ross served on the county commission to study school consolidation plans.

The revered title of "Kershaw Guards" was given to the newly commissioned National Guard unit, Battery B, 713th AAA Gun Battalion under Capt. Robert E. David. In late 1949 a new commanding officer, Lt. Col. William G. Major, Jr. , assumed leadership over Battery B. Ray C. Strickland, son of Carl and Bertha Strickland of Blaney, enlisted in Battery B and participated in the annual two-week training at Fort Stewart, Georgia in 1949.

Kershaw County Guards at Ft. Stewart, GA. 1949

In the early 40s tuberculosis was a serious health concern for the county. In 1946 an even more worrisome disease was "polio" or "infantile paralysis". Toward the end of 1947 five new cases of polio occurred in the county. A fund was started to purchase an iron lung for Camden Hospital and public health monitoring for polio, tuberculosis, and other hygiene related illnesses was stepped up. A mobile X-ray unit visited Blaney to examine patients of all ages. Free clinics identified a dozen more cases of tuberculosis. But this time there was new hope for treatment, a new TB "miracle" drug, streptomycin. Camden Hospital was thought to be too small to serve the county's ever growing population, so serious thought was given to enlarging the hospital. In 1949 the Kershaw County delegation earmarked $100,000 toward the estimated $450,000 cost to renovate Camden Hospital.

The Dixiecrat Party…

The ever smouldering issue of civil rights reared its head as the nation approached the 1948 presidential election. A tug of war existed between those in favor of ending legal racial segregation and white supremacy advocates. Kershaw County Democrats were unhappy with the national party and their endorsement for Harry Truman to be the nominee for president. They wanted a new party to hitch their wagons to in the election, a party that would favor state's rights and segregation of the races. In July, Truman was renominated by the national Democratic Party. The very next week after the Democratic Convention, Kershaw County democrats were with those that went to Birmingham, Alabama, to form a new "Dixiecrat" Party that endorsed the states rights platform. Their third party nominee for president was S. C. Governor James Strom Thurmond. The Kershaw County Democratic Executive Committee immediately endorsed Thurmond, unanimously.

Voter registration was a whole new ball of wax. The loyalty oath, which had helped the Democrats control elections since Reconstruction, was abolished by a ruling of U.S. Circuit Court Judge J. W. Waring of Charleston. The process of registering to vote in South Carolina was intimidating. A voter had to certify that he could "read and write any section of the constitution submitted to him by the registration officer or show that he owns and has paid taxes on property assessed at $300 or more". The very real possibility that "the African American vote" could carry the election was uppermost in the minds of southern political leaders.

Despite Republican expectations that Dewey would win, Harry Truman was re-elected with a substantial vote in November. Local democrats were hugely disappointed that Thurmond did not make a good showing even though he carried Kershaw County and four southern states, including South Carolina. And so the "Dixiecrats" were relegated to history but left a door open for future third party forays.

But Strom Thurmond did not "just fade away". Born in 1902 in Edgefield County, S. C., he earned a B.S. Degree from Clemson College and became a teacher in McCormick, Ridge Spring Schools in 1923. He was commissioned a second Lieutenant in the U. S. Army Reserve in 1924. He became an Edgefield attorney after passing the S. C. bar in 1930. He was elected a state senator from Edgefield County in 1932. He was a Circuit Court Judge 1938-1946.

He joined the U. S. Army after Pearl Harbor in 1941.

He landed in France on D-Day with the 82nd Airborne Div. in 1944.

He was elected Governor of South Carolina in 1946.

He ran for President as a "Dixiecrat" in 1948 winning 39 electoral votes.

He ran for U. S. Senate as a write-in candidate and won in 1954.

He retired from the U. S. Senate in 2002 after serving 48 years.

He died in 2003 at the age of 101.

The life, legacy, legend, and longevity of Strom Thurmond have made him one of the best-known, beloved, and respected of all South Carolina native sons throughout our state and nation.

Blaney RR Depot closed August 1974.
Courtesy of the Blaney-Elgin Museum & Historical Society

 **XI**

*In nothing do men more nearly
Approach the gods
Than in doing good
To their Fellowmen...
--Cicero*

Industrial Revolution

Many new businesses opened in Kershaw County in the years after the war, but one of the most important was the DuPont plant constructed in 1949. The company was considering about 25 sites in the fall of 1947 for their "Fiber A" (Orlon) plant project. That number was soon reduced to three -- Augusta, Ga., Huntsville, Ala., and Camden, S. C.

An option to buy 800 acres of land at each site was in place. During that winter DuPont officials visited each site and studied the possibilities. The Camden site seemed the most ideal since their site was in a very attractive location on the Wateree River, had excellent rail and highway transportation, and, most important, a ready supply of manpower. It didn't hurt that there were nearby textile markets that would become DuPont customers. They were greatly impressed with the business and political climate in South Carolina that welcomed major business enterprizes.

In the spring of 1948, 500 acres at the Camden site were purchased for $75,000 and in October the decision to build was sealed. In February 1949 construction began with ground-breaking ceremonies attended by Governor J. Strom Thurmond and other South Carolina dignitaries.

By June 1949, the Production Manager was named and Leland M. Jones was set to begin his 14-year tenure at the Camden DuPont Plant. (Upon his retirement in 1963, Jones would remain in the Camden area with his family. Leland Jones died June 13, 1993, at age 90.) The plant would be named in honor of Benjamin M. May, a retired Manager of Rayon. Hiring began in April 1950 for the 500 employees needed for start-up, and plans for the additional Staple (Orlon) plant were introduced. In July 1950, the first "Orlon" was spun and DuPont's investment hit $25 million.

So what is Orlon? It is a synthetic textile acrylic fiber originally intended for outdoor use in automobile tops, awnings, window coverings and other items needing strength and resistance to sunlight decomposition. Carpet and clothing also were made and successfully marketed because the acrylic fiber had good insulation qualities, was comfortable, and wrinkle resistant.

But the "Red Letter Day" was October 6, 1950, when DuPont Company President Crawford H. Greenwalt formally dedicated the new "Orlon" acrylic fiber plant at Camden, S. C. Eighty-nine state, county, and city officials were present along with 500 DuPonters from May Plant Construction and Operations. The platform was decorated with red, white, and blue bunting on a sunny, but cool day with a brisk breeze keeping "Old Glory" fluttering on its new flag pole celebrating the first full-scale commercial operation of its kind in the world. Two radio stations, WACA of Camden and WIS of Columbia, broadcast the entire program.

The year 1951 saw the start-up of the Staple Plant and in 1956 the filament production of "Orlon" discontinued with facilities converted to Orlon staple.

The year 1951 saw the start-up of the Staple Plant and in 1956 the filament production of "Orlon" discontinued with facilities converted to Orlon staple. By 1963 the Camden plant work force was about 1200, and the plant site was deemed ideal for expansion. A decision was made to build a Nylon plant at the Camden May Plant site. William F. Tripp, Jr. became the new May Plant Manager and was elected shortly after to the Kershaw County Council.

From the commercial Nylon product of 1938 that gave us ladies stockings and undergarments, to the first shipment of Nylon in 1968 from the May Plant that gave us carpets, upholstery, drapery, tire cord, and many other industrial uses, DuPont has given us a truly universal fiber.

In 1971, "Dacron" was added to the plant making this site the first "3-Fiber" plant with Orlon, Nylon, and Dacron. The "Dacron" produced at the plant is used mostly for clothing because of its unique properties, in that the fabric is very light, quick drying and wrinkle resistant. In the first five years after "Dacron," employment doubled at the plant.

Not only has the DuPont May Plant provided employment and world changing products for our county its employees have always been active in community life. They have provided leadership in churches, on school boards, county and town councils, in scout groups and service clubs. May Planters wanted what we all want - a better place to live.

DuPont May Plant 1975

On December 2, 1953, this story appeared in the local DuPont plant newsletter in an issue of the "*May Times*".

"The power of advertising when coupled with the wonders of science was shown recently when an elderly lady of Georgia sat down at her desk to write a letter. In it she said she had heard of a remarkable Orlon PLANT in South Carolina which had flourished grandly in the past several years, and had grown considerably in size from 1951 through the end of 1952. She had six good acres of Georgia soil, she wrote, which were probably as good as or better than that of South Carolina, and she wondered if she could get some seeds so she could have an Orlon PLANT of her own. We will know that science has truly triumphed when we can plant a seed that yields a 50 million dollar investment in men, money, machines, and material."

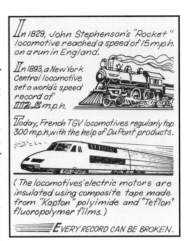

In 1829, John Stephenson's "Rocket" locomotive reached a speed of 15 m.p.h. on a run in England.

In 1893, a New York Central locomotive set a world's speed record of 112.5 m.p.h.

Today, French TGV locomotives regularly top 300 m.p.h. with the help of DuPont products.

(The locomotives' electric motors are insulated using composite tape made from "Kapton" polyimide and "Teflon" fluoropolymer films.)

Every record can be broken.

May Times Graphic

Separate but Equal...

By 1949 school consolidation had eliminated many small facilities so that only these segregated schools remained in the county: Antioch, Baron DeKalb, Bethune, Blaney, Camden, Jackson, Kirkwood, Midway, Mt. Pisgah, Pine Grove, Pine Tree Hill, and St. Matthew. The South Carolina General Assembly passed legislation that required combining South Carolina's 1630 school districts into 46, one per county. Communities protested that their identity would be lost and that their local educational needs would not be met without representation. The law mandating "separate but equal schools" required improvements be instituted in African American schools and rural schools. As an example of the disparity, modern lunchrooms were slow to appear in these schools.

The DuPont families moving into the county needed adequate schools and educational growth in the West Wateree area emerged as a thorny issue tied to industrial growth. Both Lugoff and Blaney agreed to consolidate but only if their community was the new school construction site. Post World War II high schools could offer veterans any course strong enough in demand like agricultural and industrial classes. At Blaney, "on the farm" training under A. Dowey and Agriculture teacher R. M. Richbourg included field trips.

1949 Blaney High School Graduation Class.
First class to graduate from the 12th grade.
Courtesy of Van Strickland

The 1949 Blaney High School Graduation Class picture: L-R Back Row - Clinton Goff, Thomas Goff, Ray Strickland, Claytor Campbell, Olin Goff, Marvin Campbell and Preston Goff. L-R Front Row - Ollie Dixon, Ollie Mae Branham, Betty Aldrich, Lois Branham, Evangeline Hunter and Betty Lou Dowey. Absent and not pictured Fred Duckett and William Cessar

The Kershaw County Library bookmobile was a welcome sight every two weeks in the Blaney community starting in 1949. Though the community longed for its own library that was only a dream that few believed would ever materialize

Blaney in 1949 was a community of hope. The skeleton of a huge industrial plant rising within a few miles was evidence of a long awaited prosperity that the town and surrounding community felt was a dream come true-at last. Dependent for so many years on agriculture and "King Cotton", they would not abandon this tried and true way of living even though they knew there would be lean years mixed with good years. A new Blaney High School gymnasium was dedicated in February with standing room only inside the gym. The program included the crowning of Ollie Mae Branham as Queen of Love and Beauty by the chairman of the school board of trustees, Postmaster J. Don Watson, Jr., and the master of ceremonies was a WIS Radio personality.

There seemed to be a "if we build it, they will come" atmosphere. Glenn Dowey and his daughter, Thelma Kelly, opened The Blaney Grill. E. Talmadge Bowen built a drugstore with a registered pharmacist, soda fountain, and office space for a medical doctor. Dr. Robert A. Cochran, the new town doctor, replaced Dr. William Duncan Grigsby who died in 1948 after serving as the only town physician for 42 years. Mr. Bowen built a house for Dr. Cochran and Fred Ogburn, Jr., who was the new pharmacist and also a stockholder and business manager for Mr. Bowen. Miles Cabins were updated by I. W. Bagnal, and W. Lamar Rush opened the new Midway Colony Furniture Co.

Looking around in the community in 1949 you could see the evidence of hope in action --- new cotton warehouses, cotton platforms, and Bargain (Sale) Days on Saturdays promoting various businesses, Alton B. Nelson's Station, Mrs. Mattie Watson's grocery store, T.E. Campbell's Grocery and Shell Gas, J. Mike Carns's Parts & Garage, W. H. Graddick's Dry Goods, and the Blaney ESSO station. Crowds attended the new mobile theater tent which showed "shoot-em-up" western movies nightly for 5 cents admission. The tent was divided with one side for whites and one side for blacks. Live comedy shows were enjoyed during projector changes. You could get Bugle smoking tobacco for 5 cents, candy bars for 5 cents, and a Pepsi for 5 cents.

In July, Blaney's seventh annual Fourth of July barbecue hosted by Thurston and Matt Goff and Otis and Evelyn Goff drew hundreds of people who feasted on the good food cooked and served by G. P. Monroe, Lexie Moak, J. R. Hornsby, and Joe Hornsby. They ate four to seven hundred pounds of barbecue, slaw, tomatoes, beans, and bread with iced tea, lemonade, and cake. The Goffs furnished all the food except for some cakes brought in by friends and neighbors.

Evelyn and Otis Goff, 1992 Best looking yard award

PORTRAIT PROFILE

The son of
Dr. and Mrs. Harry Alvin Cochran
The husband of
Ruth Marie Brooks

CHILDREN
Harry Brooks Cochran
Cindy Cochran Sanders
Robert Anderson Cochran Jr.
Majorie Cochran Copeland
Phoebe Cochran Palmer
Molly Cochran Steadman

DR. ROBERT ANDERSON COCHRAN
1/18/1923 - 2/11/2003

>Graduate of Ursinus College & Temple University School of Medicine.
>1941-1949 - U. S. Army Captain, Ft. Jackson final duty station.
>1949-1979 - General Practice of Medicine in Blaney-Elgin, S. C.
>1953 & 1954 - Mayor of the Town of Blaney, S. C.
>1958-1971 - Member of the Kershaw County School Board.
>Member of American Legion Post 17, Camden.
>Member of Salem United Methodist Church.

   The above facts do not reveal the depth of this country doctor who cared for young and old regardless of race or financial status. He delivered hundreds of babies and made house calls all over Kershaw, Richland and Fairfield counties. He also administered polio vaccine to local school children, served as the team doctor for the Blaney Wildcats sports teams, and occasionally cared for ailing livestock. He was known for mentoring struggling students and furnished needed school supplies and equipment. He enjoyed boating, fishing, gardening, and delighting friends and family with his humorous stories. He and his wife of 56 years, Ruth, raised their six children in Blaney-Elgin.

He is buried in Salem United Methodist Church Cemetery, Elgin, S. C.

The Middle…

Providing adequate housing with urban services and infrastructure was a frequent topic in the Blaney town council meetings. Two Mayors served during the 1950s, Dr. Robert A. Cochran and E. C. Potter, Jr. With the advent of industrial operations like the DuPont Orlon Plant in West Wateree with its large scale production and employment of local workers, Blaney knew they would have to change, in a big way, in order to grow. The most pressing need was a community water system. Men serving on the town council during this time were E. T. Bowen, Ed Campbell, J. M. Wilson, J. T. Motley, J. P. Ross, N. K. Rose, J. G. Ross, and Paul Ross, Jr. All of these men were very active in local affairs and some, like E. T. Bowen, also were known as "movers and shakers" in county-wide economic development.

The 1950 cotton season though plagued by the old nemesis, the boll weevil, carried through with traditional events which were duly reported by the local newspaper. In August 1950, the Blaney ginner E. T. Bowen bought the first bale at 514 lbs. from farmer L. P. Rose for 40 cents per lb. The corn crop was the "best ever", and tobacco did well also. Turkish tobacco was planted for the first time. Antioch was the county fair exhibit winner with Blaney coming in second, Baron DeKalb third, and Mt. Pisgah fourth. Agricultural endeavors were still the "main event" in the county, though some industrial and textile plants were enticing the young people into better paying, more stable jobs. One young man from Blaney frequently remarked to his friends, "My salary at DuPont runs into six figures….my wife and five children."

In Kershaw County, 1950 was the year they started requiring building permits for new construction in excess of $1000 outside towns and cities. In November elections, secret ballot voting was allowed for the first time. In order to vote, a male had to present a registration certificate and a poll tax receipt, a female, only the registration certificate. Three statewide constitutional amendments passed to (1) eliminate the poll tax as a voting requirement, but retain it as a revenue source, (2) to require only one registration certificate instead of multiple credentials, and (3) propose school redistricting on a statewide basis.

Members of the new Kershaw County delegation were J. Claytor Arrants, Senator, and John E. Baker and Donald Holland as Representatives. When the General Assembly next convened, 21-year- old Cassatt native Donald Holland was the youngest member of the S. C. House of Representatives.

Never on Sunday…

Sundays were traditionally for going to church in Blaney, with all the stores and businesses closed. Little else was planned for the rest of the day except that big Sunday dinner and maybe a snooze on the couch in the afternoon or a visit to relatives and friends. But the arrival of DuPont on the scene prompted the South Carolina General Assembly to pass a new law regarding Sunday work. The DuPont plant with its compulsory continuous chemical process and rotating work shifts with women on the job as well as men, required exemptions from time-and-a-half Sunday pay and from prohibition of Sunday work by women.

Of course, Sunday labor by itself was abhorant to many Blaney church-going residents who viewed it as against scriptural law. Others saw Sunday blue laws as merely legalities, or laws that were made to be broken. However, many churches were happy with the increasing numbers of new members coming into the fellowships and gladly adjusted service times to meet shift workers' schedules.

Increased interest in church-going was fueled by the March 1950 Billy Graham Crusade in Columbia. The revival meeting drew a capacity crowd of 40,000 in Carolina Stadium on Sunday, March 12, with more than 10,000 turned away. The 31-year old evangelist preached dynamic sermons and hundreds sought him out at the end of the services for counseling.

A New Kind of War...

If you were listening to the news on radio or reading any newspapers in June 1950, you knew that North Korea invaded South Korea, but you gave it little thought as you focused on all the population changes and economic upswings of the time. You also were aware later that year that DuPont was going to build another plant, only this one would be in Aiken and Barnwell counties in South Carolina and would be a nuclear "bomb" plant. Now that was an unsettling thought. The *Camden Chronicle* warned, "In the event of an atomic bomb blast, take cover in basements or underground shelters and stay there for at least 90 seconds." Also they cautioned, "A small amount of radiation outside the body is harmless, but inside the body it may cause much trouble."

All Kershaw County schools, in compliance with the S. C. Defense Act of 1950 passed by the General Assembly, would teach children to "duck and cover" in drills where they took shelter from "atomic bombs" under their desks. Some families were concerned enough about the danger to actually dig bomb shelters for protection in their back yards. Extra food, water, and first aid kits were stocked for the aftermath of the bomb blast.

The National Defense Dept., however, was convinced that the southeastern states in America would not be attacked since Soviet bombers could not fly that far from their bases. So they established large military operations in the southeast area which included the Savannah River "bomb plant" near Aiken.

The Korean War caused a call-up of the 92 men of Co. D, 122nd Batt. of Engineers and Commander Capt. W. L. Jackson to Fort Jackson for a two-week encampment. Batt. B, 713th AAA Gun Bn. under Commander First Lt. William G. Major, Jr. was federalized on August 14 after returning from a two week encampment with four officers and 137 enlisted men reporting for active duty. The Kershaw County draft was reactivated in the summer of 1950 and called men up in August. Fifty men were inducted in the first 6 months of the war. Twelve county men lost their lives in the Korean War which ended in the summer of 1953.

Hospital Advice and Dissent...

The ongoing Camden Hospital issues added one more notch to the belt when, in 1954, a Charleston bond attorney informed the Hospital Board Chairman, John Carl West, that the board might not be legally constituted to authorize spending. The eleven board members were composed of two representatives from the Medical Society, one each from the Farm Bureau, Hospital Auxiliary, Ministerial Association, County Board of Directors, County Delegation, and one each from the town councils of Bethune, Blaney, Camden, and Kershaw.

The seventy-six-year-old county-wide hospital was afflicted with growing pains. Dealing with new medical insurance companies like Blue Cross-Blue Shield, which many DuPont families used, and just "keeping up with the times" strained hospital personnel. The need for modern equipment, more beds and operating rooms, plus the lack of isolation wards and maternity rooms threatened public health and having to turn away patients in need was a real possibility.

Though nearly everyone agreed a new hospital was the real answer, political party influences had time and again delayed the issuance of bonds for a new hospital, and disagreements between Democrats tied up funding for county supplies as well as hospital operating expenses. Finally the SC General Assembly passed a Kershaw County bond bill which Governor James F. Byrnes vetoed, but the General Assembly overrode the veto 97-2. After more "spirited" dissent, plans emerged for a new 80-bed, $1,250,000 hospital. Four years later (1958), the new, modern Kershaw County Memorial Hospital opened on Roberts Street in Camden.

Camden Hospital, Camden S.C.
Courtesy of the Camden Archives

John Carl West, whose interest in the hospital issues got him started on a long career in public service, made his first political speech at Blaney in a 1954 county election campaign tour. The May 28 *Camden Chronicle* reported that a large crowd heard him refer to the recent Supreme Court decision, "Brown vs. Board of Education": "Seven days ago a group of men in Washington put upon the South the greatest problem we have been faced with since 1876. By an edict of a court sitting in Washington, it has been determined that our children cannot go to segregated schools. The solution to that problem will rest on the shoulders of the men you send to the legislature. I cannot offer you a wrapped-up solution to this problem, but I can tell you that I will work with all the talents at my command to see that the races are not mixed in our schools." In time, West would become a moderate and would work toward unifying the races.

U. S. history was made in 1954 when Strom Thurmond, former Governor of South Carolina, was the first person elected to a major national office on a write-in ballot. He ran against Democratic nominee Edgar Brown to fill the U. S. Senate seat vacated by the death of Burnett Maybank. Kershaw County voters favored Thurmond 2-1.

In 1954 Robert A. Cochran was not only the town physician, but was elected mayor, too. His council was E. T. Bowen, Ed Campbell, J.M. Wilson and J. T. Motley. Decisions made were to retain a town lawyer (DeLoach, Camden), appoint E. T. Bowen to the Kershaw County Hospital Board to replace Dr. R. A. Cochran, change council meeting day to every second Tuesday of each month, and elect J. M. Wilson as the mayor pro tem. They also voted to install outside location lights at nine locations to include Blaney Lumber Mill, Dr. R. A. Cochran corner, Salem Methodist Church, hardware store, back of Blaney Baptist Church, Mrs. Corrie Sanders, B. K. Rose & C. R. Bowen homes, back of the school house, and Bob Garrison's place.

In 1956 President Dwight D. Eisenhower was re-elected President of the United States. Richard M. Nixon was his Vice President. The war-time general of the armies had gained the approval of the country during his first term which started in 1952. He was the first president to be limited to two terms in office and was popular due to the Federal Highway Act which had proved to be a boon to the U. S. economy. The average worker in the country was making $3600 a year in 1956. The 1950s proved to be a period of prosperity in Blaney.

Blaney Public School 1950

Blaney We Have Loved Thee…

Disasters come in many forms, and they usually happen when we least expect them. Sudden, fatal vehicle accidents are dreaded, but the most fearful of all is fire--uncontrolled, destructive fire.

Every year the high school commencement for Blaney High School was usually held near the end of May. Class Day exercises were always a time of great expectation for graduating seniors who would receive their school awards for scholastic achievements, and school yearbooks would be passed around for students to sign and write "goodbye" remarks. These exercises were held in the school auditorium for the entire student body, and the program included speeches by teachers and graduating seniors and ended with the school's Alma Mater. The graduation ceremonies were in the evening, sometimes on the same day as Class Day exercises or the next day. In 1956 the graduation and Class Day exercises were scheduled for Wednesday, May 30.

But a tragic accident changed that plan. Early Wednesday morning a student school-bus driver was moving a bus forward to a gas pump when someone shouted for him to stop. He did, but too late--the rear wheel of the bus had run over a little 2-year-old girl who died instantly. The driver never saw the child who had been playing in front of the bus. She lived just a few feet away. Her father was the school Agriculture teacher, and their home was on the school grounds. The teacher was in Alabama at the time making arrangements for the family to move there. The entire community was shocked and upset over the incident, and Blaney school officials delayed the graduation ceremonies until Friday, June 1.

The tragedy cast a pall over the graduation festivities, but the graduation took place as rescheduled on June 1 in the school auditorium. The salutatorian, Jimmie Dillard, gave the traditional welcoming speech. The valedictory speech was by Shelba Wooten. Diplomas were given out and congratulations offered to the twelve graduates by Supt. Edward W. Shingler. The graduates were Helen Barfield, Annette Branham, Betty Goff, Floyd Goff, Gary Goff, Jr., Virginia Guest, Margaret Jackson, Nettie Moak, Jimmy Nelson, Jimmie Rose, and Shelba Wooten. About 375 people attended the graduation exercises which were over by 9:00 PM. The graduates were told to return in the morning (Saturday) for their report cards.

In the early morning hours, around 5:00 AM, a motorist, J. F. Ingle of Columbia, was passing by the school on U.S. Hwy. #1, on his way to go fishing, when he noticed a large fire in the school. He pulled over and stopped at Judge Alton Nelson's house and awakened Mrs. Maude Nelson. She called the Camden Fire Dept. The firemen arrived around 5:45 AM and found the 2-story school building ready to collapse, engulfed in flames. The flames were seen first at the north end of the building and in less than an hour had spread throughout the building. For a time as the fire burned, explosions could be heard as drums of inflammables ignited and exploded. On the second floor, in the Science Room area, a huge explosion lifted the roof completely off the building. The Blaney School principal, John Krantz, attempted to enter the building to save some school records, but the fire and heat prevented an entrance.

Camden firemen were able to save the new cafeteria behind the school though windows facing the burning school were cracked and the roof was damaged. The gymnasium, butcher pen, cannery, and an isolated classroom were not damaged by the flames. Two pianos, some furniture and the podium were removed from the auditorium before the flames claimed the scene of the previous night's commencement program.

The Chairman of the Blaney School Board of Trustees, J. D. Watson, Sr., was one of the first to arrive at the fire and believed the blaze could have started an hour earlier than its detection.

The huge fire completely destroyed the entire grammar and high school and the school auditorium. Report cards along with all school books and records were also consumed in the fire. Since the town had no fire department or town water system, they had to rely on the Camden Fire Dept. who were, at best, 30 minutes away. The fire not only burned the main brick school but threatened the town business district and nearby homes as well.

The dawn brought shock and disbelief as townspeople viewed the smoking ruins. Parts of the brick walls were like black spikes poking into the early morning light amid charred embers in a big black hole where the entrance to the building used to be. The seniors showing up to get their report cards were overwhelmed by the horrible sight of what had been the night before a scene of joy. They held one another and cried against the stark reality of the unthinkable.

Supt. Shingler said that nothing was saved from the building and that all school records were lost (with the exception of 3 sets of permanent student records). Twelve typewriters and all athletic equipment was also lost. A valuable water system installed in the current school year was totally destroyed. He placed the value of the loss of the building and its contents at $500,000.

The shock of it all was unrelenting in its scope when the community realized that 155 high school, and 276 elementary school pupils were now without a school, 21 teachers now had no place to teach, and the community had lost their only educational facility which had originally been built in 1915. County Supt. Of Education, Arthur Stokes, promised that the school would be rebuilt and that temporary buildings would be used until funds were made available to rebuild.

The County Sheriff, D. E. Hilton, Fire Chief Carl Hammond, SLED Chief Brady, and insurance company authorities conducted an investigation in the days following the fire, and much to the dismay and astonishment of the community, Supt. Shingler was taken into custody on Wednesday, June 6 on an open charge and was being held in the Kershaw County jail pending further investigation.

After being held about a week, Shingler was charged with breach of trust in a warrant signed by Sheriff Hilton. The warrant issued by Judge Charles Blyther charged that Shingler did "feloniously take, misappropriate and fraudulently appropriate the money ($2000 belonging to the school, PTA, Junior and Senior classes, lunchroom and other students) to his own use." The judge set the bond for Shingler at $5000. Shingler was released from jail when his bond was put up by bondsman P. L. McCall of Darlington on Thursday, June 13.

Word was received around June 15 that B. E. Livingston, a former teacher at Baron DeKalb school and twice Superintendent at Antioch school, had resigned his position in the Laurens school system to accept the superintendent position at Blaney.

On Thursday, Oct. 11, 1956, Shingler was arrested in Orangeburg with new charges brought against him for unlawful burning of a building. He was returned to Camden and lodged in the Kershaw County jail. The arrest came after further investigation was conducted by the county Sheriff's department, state SLED office, and the state Fire Marshall's office.

On Oct. 19, Judge Blyther ruled that the state had made a proper case against Shingler, and he passed the case on to higher court. The decision came after a preliminary hearing was conducted Thursday, Oct. 18, in which three witnesses testified, Robert Carswell, partner in Robert A. Bruce Co. auditing firm of Camden; County Sheriff D. E. Hilton; and O. L. Newman, Blaney School janitor. Carswell told the court that $1,327 was missing and unaccounted for in auditing the school's account. The money was missing from the school's activity fund which was reported to have been in the safe. The money was reported burned in the fire by Shingler.

Sheriff Hilton said Shingler told him on the morning after the fire that he had personally locked the safe the afternoon prior to the fire and that he was the last to leave the school the night of the fire along with his wife, two children, and another couple. The Sheriff also testified that the safe was found on the morning after the fire lying face down and open. The door was off the safe which was a hinge type door easily removed. The door had not been torn loose or pried off. The safe was empty. Also discovered at the scene were several cans near the gasoline pump north of the building.

O. L. Newman told the court that he had been janitor at the school since October 1955 and that an investigating officer had found a small kerosene can and a larger can near a stairway. The investigator asked him if he had seen either of them prior to the fire. He had never seen them before.

Assistant State Solicitor John Ford stated that the purpose of the hearing was not to determine the guilt or innocence of Shingler but merely to present the State's case. He summed up the hearing by saying that, "Shingler had a motive for the charges. (1) School was closing down, (2) the books showed a $1300 deficit, and (3) the auditors report was due soon. He had overdrawn bank accounts and outstanding bills, and it was not logical he would have left money in the safe since he had made a bank deposit only a few days before the fire. Also the fact that he was the only one who knew the combination of the safe and had personally locked the safe the day before and the safe being found open with the door off the day after the fire. Coupled with the cans found near the gasoline pump and under the stairs. These facts support the charges against him."

Clint T. Graydon, Shingler's Columbia attorney, requested the charges be dismissed. Judge Blyther delayed his decision one day to consider all the evidence and Graydon's request. The next day the judge denied Graydon's request. He stated that the Grand Jury would have to act on the case before it could go on to General Sessions Court.

On Tuesday, Oct. 23, 1956, the Grand Jury true-billed charges against Shingler, but because of a heavy docket he would not be tried in this term of court. He faced four charges on the court calendar.
(1) Breach of trust.
(2) Grand larceny.
(3) Embezzlement.
(4) Unlawful burning of a building or arson.

The Shingler case was on the court docket to be tried on February 18, 1957, but was carried over to the next term of court because John Krantz, a principal witness, was ill with influenza.

The June 1957 term of court docket showed the Shingler case to be tried on June 26, but the case had to be postponed until the next court date due to the illness of Judge G. Duncan Bellinger of Columbia.

The November 1957 court docket had the Shingler case scheduled but it was carried over to the next court term due to the illness of a chief witness, Shelba Wooten, who was ill with influenza.

On February 17, 1958, Judge Littlejohn ordered that the trial be carried over to the next term of court due to the illness of the chief counselor for the defense, Clint Graydon. On May 19, 1958, the Shingler trial was scheduled to be tried, but the defense attorney, Clint Graydon, was ill. The case was postponed again.

Finally, on the October 27, 1958 court docket the Shingler case came up for trial. The trial, postponed five times since Shingler was indicted in October 1956, began and was expected to last several days. The state had 20 witnesses ready to testify, and the defense had 12 standing by. Seating the jury consumed most of the first days of the trial with 12 jurors chosen. Court Clerk Edward Ogburn arraigned Shingler on the charges and asked, "How do you plead?" Shingler answered in a firm voice, "Not Guilty." Shingler's attorneys, father and son, Clint Graydon and C. T. Graydon, opened the trial with an attempt to quash the indictment saying the charges were not substantiated and were not properly joined. Judge George Gregory overruled both motions and the trial proceeded.

Solicitor Pou Taylor called Robert A. Carswell as the state's first witness to testify as to the audit of the Blaney School Activities Funds. The audit revealed that $1,314.35 was unaccounted for and that Shingler had generally agreed that the audit was correct. He also found that Shingler had on a number of occasions written personal checks on the "school activities" account. Kershaw County Supt. of Education Arthur Stokes testified that on several occasions he had to prod Shingler into making payments on bills the school owed and that several months after the school burned he had paid $4000 on Blaney school accounts.

The state continued to construct a web of circumstantial evidence against Shingler as they presented witnesses testifying that Shingler had stated in their presence that "the school's going to burn down." One witness said she had found $200 hidden in an outhouse at the rear of the Shingler home following the fire. Mrs. Shelba Wooten Mattox testified concerning the funds collected by the students in 1955-56 and the discrepancy between funds turned over to Shingler and his lack of accounting for $700 in the Senior Class Trip account. She said, "Student complaints and talk about the situation prompted Shingler to call the Junior and Senior Classes together and tell them if the talk did not cease he would sue them for slander." John Krantz testified about the electrical system in the school saying everything was fine and that there had not been enough money to get the school annuals out of the depot upon arrival a week before the fire.

Third grade teacher, Mrs. Sally Koon, testified that she knew of no wiring trouble in the school and that Shingler appeared to be distraught and shaken in the closing weeks of school. On one occasion he came into her classroom which was across the hall from his office and buried his face in his hands and said desperately, "Mrs. Koon, Mrs. Koon, what are we going to do?"

She said she responded, "Nothing," because she did not understand what he was referring to. She also said that there had been dissension among the school trustees that spring over the rehiring of Shingler.

W. G. Munn, Blaney upholsterer, testified that Shingler had paid him for personal jobs by taking money out of the funds kept in the school office. C. W. Wooten testified that he had joined a conversation on graduation night in which Shingler said that the wiring was in bad condition and the school was going to burn down. Walter Rhame, a registered electrician working as maintenance supervisor for the Kershaw County Schools, took the stand to say that he had made five or six trips to the Blaney School and had installed a new breaker system to take care of overloaded lines. He felt that after the breaker box was installed the school was "reasonably safe" or as safe as any of the older school buildings in the county system.

The statement Shingler had given at SLED headquarters in Columbia after his initial arrest was entered into evidence in which Shingler said he had placed between $1500 and $2000 in the safe before the fire. He said he hadn't paid for the annuals because many of the students had not paid for theirs and some wanted to see the annual before ordering. He said the publishers were not supposed to send the annuals COD. He said the school's electrical fixtures and the furnace were in a bad state of repairs. While Shingler was at SLED he called his wife, and the telephone call was monitored by SLED. On the basis of what Shingler told his wife in the conversation they then began to question him about money being hidden in an outhouse. Shingler then admitted he was about $150 to $200 short on money.

Sheriff Hilton testified of the condition of the safe after the fire and brought the safe into the courtroom to introduce as evidence. He also told the court that Shingler's eyelashes and eyebrows were singed and that Shingler stated that flying sparks must have singed him. The Sheriff found $99 in school funds in Shingler's house after the fire, and he said Mrs. Shingler voluntarily turned in a small amount of additional school funds later.

The long-delayed trial of Edward W. Shingler abruptly ended with a dramatic turn at 12:30 PM on Wednesday, November 5, 1958. The defendant switched his plea to "Guilty" on the count of breach of trust with fraudulent intent and stood quietly as Judge George Gregory sentenced him to four years imprisonment. In pronouncing sentence, Judge Gregory told Shingler that he could have gotten from three months to ten years for the offence. He said he felt that on the basis of the evidence the jury would have been obligated to convict him not only on the breach of trust count but the burning charge as well.

The sudden turn of events happened as a result of a deal cut during a court recess where the defendant agreed to plead guilty on the first count of the indictment provided the remaining counts of embezzlement and burning of a public building against him were dropped. The state accepted these terms.

The last witness before the recess was Mrs. Shingler who said she knew nothing about any wrongdoing on her husband's part.

Judge Gregory stated that in pronouncing the four-year sentence, he did so with full recognition of the fact that the defendant and his family had already suffered and would continue to suffer the results of his crime.

ALMA MATER

BLANEY we have loved thee
From our childhood days
The golden hours we cherished
In study, work and play.

Ere we leave thy dear walls
We will lift our hearts in praise
May the richest, tenderest blessings
Rest on thee always.

CHORUS
BLANEY HIGH, BLANEY HIGH
For thee we'll always stand
BLANEY HIGH, BLANEY HIGH
The dearest in the land.

Words by Doris Maddox
(Senior Year at Blaney High School 1939-1940)
Music by Kenneth Baldwin
(Music teacher at Blaney High School 1939-1940)

Segregation Forever…

As national pressures increased to end segregation of the schools, local citizens voiced dissent in various ways. Newspapers quoted only African American residents, who were in favor of continued segregation. The dormant Ku Klux Klan emerged seeking new members throughout the county. The NAACP had planning meetings urging voter registration. Political interest revived as the legal processes made it clear that segregation in the South would soon end. Folks repeated the old adage that "The South is a place; east, west, or north are only directions." That might partly explain their problems with wanting to remain in the "status quo" and not wanting to move forward toward an unknown though perhaps better future. In 1956 the schools were still segregated, and many hoped they would stay that way.

Into Space and Beyond…

In 1957 our vocabulary was enlarged as we learned that the Soviet Union had launched a space satellite named "Sputnik". All of a sudden everybody wanted to be educated in space jargon. New emphasis was placed on schools to add foreign languages, develop achievement tests, be proficient in math, science, and well, "everything." Americans wanted to explore space, too, and parents paid more attention to their children's classwork, homework, and extra curricular activities. SCETV was a pioneer in classroom television which revolutionized teaching and was helpful during teacher shortages as well.

Speaking of revolutions, the industrial revolution in West Wateree continued after DuPont came in the form of another "Yankee" move to the South. The Sand Hills had often been a curse in the past, but it had its upside, too. After three years of negotiating, a 124-year-old New York State industrial sands and foundry materials firm announced they would be building a $300,000 sand foundry on a 392-acre tract located between Lugoff and Blaney. Whitehead Brothers Sand Company started production in 1958. Manager Lester Tomlin said the company had recognized and appreciated the fine clay and sand in the Blaney area.

The Kershaw County Superintendent's promise to rebuild Blaney School began to come to fruition in July 1957 when it was announced that state funds were being made available and the school would be ready by September 1958. The first allotment of $50,000 would begin the project with an expected $352,000 needed to complete the school. The 1957-58 school year would be taught in temporary portable classrooms. Ira Goff and Edward Hornsby were appointed to the Blaney School Board of Trustees.

The 1957-58 Blaney School Faculty was announced in September 1957.
They were B. E. Livingston, Superintendent and John A. Krantz, Principal.
Teachers were Mae Plumley, Sally Y. Koon, Paul Ross, Jr., Mary Eva Bruce, Annie H. Able, Mr. A. J. Smith, Jeannie Dill Hester, Evelyn D. Horne, Sallie S. McGee, Jesse David Crawford, Ethel Mae Bruce, Elizabeth H. Ross, Ernest P. Clyburn, Irene Pellum, John A. Riley, Joanne P. Strickland (Music) and William Burns (Band). Jimmie D. Rose (Secretary); Owen Lloyd (Custodian); Maude C. Nelson (Lunchroom Mgr.); Sallie B. Watts and Doris M. Fulmer (Assts.). Bus Drivers were - Marion Crenshaw, Leroy Fortner, Paul Kirkland, Jack Perry, Hazel Reynolds, and Finland Watts.

Blaney School 1958

 **XII**

When speculation has done its worst,
Two and two still make four.
--Samuel Johnson

From Whistle Stop to Stop Watch

In 1960-61 we had, for the first time, a television-run election for President of the United States between Richard Nixon and John F. Kennedy. Though television was in its infancy (in Blaney), it captured the nation's attention, and we would forever more be changed. The election was won by John Fitzgerald Kennedy and we would follow him "to Camelot" by television through the Cold War, his space program, the Peace Corps, the Bay of Pigs fiasco, the Cuban missile crisis, the erection of the Berlin Wall, civil rights and racial tensions, and finally, we would witness the awful tragedy of his assassination in 1963.

Time For Elgin...

From the DuPont success story of the 50s, Blaney officials could see visible improvements in the town's physical appearance--new homes and sub-divisions springing up, local business growth, population increasing, more vehicle traffic, and the spin-off needs for more community infrastructure, fire and police protection, and expansion of streets and roads. Local leaders had long felt that the lack of a municipal water system was holding up the town's progress.

In 1961, Mayor E. C. Potter, Jr., with Council Members Norman K. Rose, Dan Kelly, T. Ed Campbell, and Carroll R. Bowen, determined to assess and address the issues impeding town growth. John Carl West, who was a State Senator for Kershaw County as well as the Blaney town attorney at the time, put town officials in contact with state officials who were trying to connect industries looking for sites with communities hoping to attract new business opportunities. Governor Ernest "Fritz" Hollings's administration advised there was a company looking for a site, "The Elgin National Watch Company" of Elgin, Illinois. John Carl West acted as the go-between in the negotiations with the watch company.

The National Watch Company of Chicago, Illinois, was incorporated on August 27, 1864, with a capital of $100,000. The company moved to Elgin, Illinois, and was reorganized on April 25, 1865, with a capital of $500,000. The first watch made was an 18 size, key-wind and full-plate with quick-train and straight-line escapement arranged to set on the face and adjusted to temperature. It was named the Benjamin W. Raymond (in honor of one of the founders of the company). It took six months to complete and sold for $117 at a time when pork chops cost 3 cents per lb. (At an auction several years ago, the watch was bought for $15,000.) On May 12, 1874, the name of the company was changed to "The Elgin National Watch Company". In 1888 the watch factory was producing 7500 watches per week with 2300 employees. Men earned $3.00 a day, women $6.00 per week for a 6-day workweek.

In World War I, the U. S. Army had the Elgin factory train 350 men to make precision repairs required in battlefields. In World War II, all civilian work stopped, and Elgin fulfilled military contracts. Post-war the company diversified making decorator clocks, transistor radios, and wedding rings, but its heart beat was the Elgin watch.

The world's largest watch manufacturing complex was located in several buildings in Illinois from its inception in 1864 and was now proposing to move its entire fine-jeweled watch production to South Carolina.

Blaney could not believe their good fortune that this company was considering locating in a lowly "whistle-stop." Senator West met with the company officials and persuaded them to take a look at Blaney. The company indicated they wanted to be located near a good labor supply, and they were impressed with Blaney's spacious site and close proximity to Columbia. As the watch company officials surveyed the proposed site a loaded hint was dropped. They said the one thing they hated about leaving Elgin, Illinois was that the watch bore the name of the town and it was a great advertisement. Sen. West replied, "We'll see about that."

Charlie Wooten, who would later be mayor (1971-1979) of Elgin, played an important role on the local level in getting the company to settle in Blaney. He said one of the watch company executives told him that the name change didn't have anything to do with why the company made the move to Blaney, and that "They would have come here anyway."

During the eight months of negotiations, Sen. West worked tirelessly to bring a new industry to his hometown region. His collaboration with O. Stanley Smith, Chairman of the S. C. Technical Education Committee of the State Development Board, was an instrumental factor.

Elgin Watch Plant, Elgin, S.C.

By July 4, 1962, the *Camden Chronicle* announced to the world, "New Industry Coming to Kershaw County". Blaney residents knew what it would mean to them if the watch plant came, and so they took the unusual step of buying the 87-acre site the company had selected to give to them, gratis. Wooten said, "It was an enticement to get them to come, and we doubted they would buy it ---they didn't have any money, and they were coming here for cheap labor. That was the beginning of foreign competition, and they were getting hit hard."

The combined efforts of Charlie Wooten and E. Talmadge Bowen brought in $10,000 for the purchase of the land. But they were $2000 short. By September, Doyle Cannon, Manager of Carolina Power and Light Co., offered to pay the balance. The citizens who gave money to purchase the land were:

Mrs. Roberta M. Rose	Lemuel W. Wooten
Francis E. "Pete" James	R. W. Coker
Mrs. J. M. Wilson	Boykin K. Rose
E. L. "Shorty" Sessions	Cranshaw Branham
J. A. Kelly	J. Don Watson, Jr.
Charlie W. Wooten	J. R. Hornsby
Clyde M. Boykin	Hazel W. Smith
Alton B. Nelson	T. Ed Campbell
E. Talmadge Bowen	Eddie Ross
J. Paul Ross, Jr.	Miles Grocery
Claude E. Campbell	Carolina Power & Light Co.
John Mike Carns	Robert M. Cochran, M.D.
Ernest C. Potter, Jr.	

The ground breaking for the new $1 million watch assembly plant at Blaney was held on September 4, 1962, with Governor Ernest F. Hollings and Elgin Watch Co. President Henry M. Margolis wielding the shovels while M. B. Kahn, contractor for Southern Construction Co., Rep. L. P. Branham, Charlie Wooten, E. Talmadge Bowen, Sen. John C. West, Rep. Donald Holland, Frank Rector of the Kershaw County Chamber of Commerce, and Blaney Mayor Ernest C. Potter, Jr. looked on. About 200 people attended the ceremonies and there was great excitement about the new 70,000 sq. ft. plant which would initially employ 240 employees. When the applications were counted, 1500 people had applied for the 240 jobs.

After the ground breaking, the move to change the name of the town began in earnest with Mayor E. C. Potter, Sen. John C. West, and E. T. Bowen leading the way. A petition signed by the majority of the town freeholders for a referendum vote was approved, and a special election date of October 9, 1962 was set to legally decide the issue. Only the people living within the town limits were allowed to vote, and there were less than 100 residents with only 90 registered to vote.

The question on the ballot was to be answered yes or no. "Shall the charter of the Town of Blaney be amended to change the name of said town from Blaney to Elgin?" The ballots were printed by Davis Printing Co. of Camden, and the signers of the election notice were the Commissioners of Election for Kershaw County - Joseph Upchurch, W. B. Catoe, and Fred N. Gay.

The place of the election was Judge Alton B. Nelson's office on October 9, 1962. The vote was 61 in favor of changing the name of the town to Elgin and 16 against. A total of 77 votes out of a possible 90 registered to vote. It was a 5-1 victory for all who worked so hard to get the watch plant to come to "Elgin".

Some believe that had the entire Blaney community been allowed to vote, the name of the town would have remained Blaney, and there certainly was opposition to the name change from the 1000 residents of the unincorporated community of Elgin in Lancaster County.

The two "Elgins" were only 45 miles apart, and the Elgin in Lancaster County complained that South Carolina already had an Elgin, which was named for the same company. The Lancaster town had served as a train depot and was named for the depot agent's Elgin railroad watch. They believed that having two Elgins would complicate everyone's lives. They hoped Blaney would call their town New Elgin or perhaps, Elginville.

On October 18, 1962, Secretary of State O. Frank Thornton issued an order changing the name of the town from Blaney to Elgin. He also issued a certificate amending the original charter of Blaney.

Training in watchmaking skills began October 23 in the Blaney gym which had been converted into a state technical training school. Wade Martin was the state coordinator and Marlen Bender, Chief Industrial Engineer of the Elgin Watch Co., took the lead in teaching the highly exacting trade to the 167 women finally hired for the assembly work. A crew of five men made up the original maintenance crew. Production began February 4, 1963, with Nicholas R. Marcurio as plant manager.

"Blaney-Elgin" had never seen a celebration like the Dedication Ceremony on Sunday, March 10, 1963. At 3:00 PM, 5000-7000 people showed up at the Elgin Watch plant ready to "party." In attendance were Master of Ceremonies Sen. John C. West, newly-elected Governor Donald S. Russell, U. S. Senator Strom Thurmond, former Gov. Ernest F. Hollings, U.S. Rep. Robert Hemphill, and a host of Elgin Watch Co. executives headed up by Henry M. Margolis, Board Chairman of the company. Elgin watches were given to all S. C. officials and the new employees of the plant. Sen. West was given the first watch produced at the new plant "for his numerous contributions to facilitate the company move." Rev. Dean Clyde, Pastor of Blaney Baptist Church, gave the Invocation. Rev. Milton McGuirt, Pastor of Salem Methodist Church, delivered the Benediction. The music of the Camden High School Band entertained, conducted by W.A. Basden, Director. A tour of the plant was conducted, and punch and cookies were enjoyed by all.

Town officials had long known that the lack of a municipal water system was detrimental to any industrial progress in the area, and so the Elgin Watch Co. decision to locate in Blaney forced a $250,000 water system investment by the town. And thanks to the new Elgin Watch Co., "Elgin" became the first town in the United States to receive an Economic Development grant under the new John F. Kennedy administration.

By January 1963, Elgin was drilling wells, and by February the Elgin Watch plant began production.

Good News - Bad News...

In all the "headline grabbing" news about the watch plant we do not want to fail to record the very impressive new post office facility built in 1961-62 and opened on February 7, 1962, on Church Street in "Elgin". J. Don Watson, Jr. was the Postmaster and worked in a spacious 1300 sq. ft. interior with a 108 sq. ft. platform and a paved area of 3400 sq. ft. His wife, Jean Watson, worked there with him, and Elgin can thank government officials Sen. Olin D. Johnston, Sen. Strom Thurmond, and Rep. Albert Watson for their help in making this building possible.

Postmaster Don Watson and Jean Watson 1984 Post office
Courtesy of Jean Watson

In the fall of 1967, the Hardwicke Chemical Co. broke ground on a 15-acre site near Elgin on Larry Jeffers Road. The founders of the privately owned company were Dr. James E. Hardwicke and Wilheim Frings. Sales were $25-50 million, and they employed 100-250 employees. Their business was a large scale custom manufacture of organic chemicals for the chemical industry. They moved in without much fanfare, but their professionalism and safety standards were impressive. The company was sold in 2007 to WeylChem, Inc. of International Chemical Investors GmbH. They employ 100-200 employees.

As early as May 1965, the *Wall Street Journal* reported that the Elgin Watch Co.'s move to Blaney was an expense cutting program. In 1966, the company declared an $8,354,739 loss in 1965 sales. In his dedicatory address in 1963, the Elgin Watch Co. President Henry Margolis said that the new modern watch assembly plant would be able to better compete with the onslaught of low cost foreign watches flooding the American market. He said the company had been forced to use imported movements in certain watch models to compete with low-cost foreign labor. He expressed determination not to forfeit the American jeweled watch business to foreign countries.

Early in 1967, signs of company distress became evident in layoffs at the plant and cutting back on certain things. By September, the bad news was made public. Jerome W. Robins, new company president of the Watch Co. announced the company would be phasing out its watch manufacturing operations in the U. S. "We have been most pleased with our Elgin South Carolina operation," Robins told the *Camden Chronicle*. "Our employees performed extremely well and were able to accomplish things once thought impossible in the watch industry. The decision to phase out was based on various economic factors which placed the company in a position where it could no longer manufacture movements domestically that could compete economically with imported movements of comparable qualities."

The plant was sold by the Elgin Watch Co. to the B. F. Goodrich Co. which would manufacture tennis shoes.

Many believe that the Elgin Watch Co. left because the 5-year tax exemption in Kershaw County had expired, but the facts don't support this theory. The exemption had not expired, nor was it exclusionary. In fact, the company left after four years, not five. In South Carolina, it is customary for all new industries to get a five year tax exemption, but the exemption does not keep industries from paying larger school taxes.

The Elgin Watch Company no longer exists. The Elgin name was sold to Waltham Watches. A short-lived petition was circulated to change the town's name back to Blaney, but it never really got anywhere.

What's in a name? Our children go to Blaney Elementary School. We get fire protection from the Blaney Fire Department. We attend Blaney Baptist Church. There are more than 20 Elgin named businesses in the current telephone directory. Our teenagers go to Lugoff-Elgin High School, we get water from the Lugoff-Elgin Water Authority, and some local subdivisions carry the name of Blaney as well as Elgin.

It's been 50 years since the name change. The town population in 1960 was 100. The latest 2010 census population is 1311.

Some 1963 Elgin Town Council actions included the $78,524 sale of bonds for the 1963 water system, a pay raise for the town clerk to $25.00 a month, and a decision to start reading water meters in town on May 25 with the first water bills (45) to be sent out in June. Private water pump owners were instructed by the Kershaw County Health Dept. to cut and plug all pump lines. Deposits on water meters were set at $5.00. W. D. Corder was hired as the town maintenance man for the water system with Jack Chestnut hired as his helper.

Mayor E. C. Potter, Jr. resigned on May 2, 1963, and T. Ed Campbell was appointed acting mayor until an election could be held. J. Don Watson, Jr. was elected mayor in 1964.

It had been nearly 10 years since the disastrous Blaney School fire which made it abundantly clear that the community needed its own fire department. Fund raisers were started in 1964 to pay for a town fire truck which cost $10,693. A final push for funds was made at a town barbecue dinner hosted by E. C. Potter, Sarah Emanuel, Nick Bowen, Eva Bowen, and the Elgin Watch Plant officials. The county chipped in $1500. The fire truck was ordered from W. S. Darley & Co., out of Melrose Park, Illinois. E. C. Potter, Jr. was appointed as the first fire chief of the new Blaney Fire Department.

The Drag City Races…

Elgin --1968--Drag Racing. Put them altogether and you have (drum roll) The Blaney(not Elgin) Drag Strip opened in the spring of 1968 by Ed and Sandra Smith, but there is a story before that. Beginning in 1961, Ed had used road equipment from his construction business to build a drag strip. It was "OK", but the cars just got faster and faster and the track got smaller and smaller, so in 1965 he closed the track and later teamed up with Lemuel Wooten in converting the property into a housing subdivision named "Tall Pines". He also purchased 300 acres of land in the Elgin area between White Pond and Green Hill Roads and designed what would become one of the top five quarter-mile drag strips in the Southeast.

In November of 1963, Jan and Dean Torrence wrote a song that would become a big hit with drag racing fans, "Drag City". The song pretty much described what went on at drag races, and fans would shout "Burn up that quarter mile!"-- just like the song, or "You're looking real tough!"-- just like the song. But you would really just have to be there to understand the dedication some fans gave to this drag strip.

Blaney Drag Strip was sanctioned by the National Hod Rod Association (NHRA); in fact, it was the only quarter mile NHRA sanctioned strip in South Carolina, and Ed and Sandra Smith knew how to make it attractive for the big-name racers to come, and they featured the annual year-end Dixie Finals and many other great match races in its prime.

In its second season the track record of 173 mph was shattered. Time and speed records continued to fall as the season went on. The first racer to run over 200 mph was a local man, Don Powell. National Champ "TV Tommy" Ivo drove his Dodge-powered rail 205 mph in 7.03 seconds, and "Big Daddy" Don Garlits ran a 7.05 sec. qtr. mile, setting a new track speed of 214.18 mph.

Although the noise and traffic annoyed local area residents some, the drag strip "brought a lot of attention and money to the community" according to Sandra Smith. The Smiths leased the track in 1976 and closed it in 1985 as an alternative to a major investment to provide needed upgrades.

Since there was a demand in the area for affordable housing, the Smiths converted this property into Blaney Hills mobile home subdivision. The streets in the development were named for the drag strip's most successful drivers. If you were to visit the drag strip location today you would find portions of the strip and pits and neatly lettered race-great names on mailboxes - Liberman Lane, Ivo Circle, Garlits Drive, and Platt Drive.

The bleachers are gone, but the earthen beams on which they sat are still there. The strip surface pavement is gone, but the land is still level and flat. Close your eyes and you can re-live the days when "A Blue Coral wax job sure looked pretty".

More Than a Postmaster…

J. Don Watson, Jr. had a lot of great things going for him, but the greatest was Jean, his wife, who aided him in all of his life's work. He was best known for his job as postmaster of Elgin from 1965 to 1987. He was mayor of the town in 1964-1965 and fire chief of the town fire dept. in 1971. He was a life-long member of Blaney Baptist Church, and he knew everybody and everybody knew him.

He was fond of telling the Blaney story to any and all who would listen and left the following notes for this historian to tell:

"My grandfather, Ed Flaherty, ran a grocery store and meat market. He killed his cows and hogs on Thursday and sold the meat on Friday and Saturday. He also bought and sold cows, mules and horses. He would go through the countryside in a horse and buggy with those for sale or trade tied in back. He always had in the buggy two cigar boxes filled with pocket knives. He said if you could trade knives with someone, you could trade animals with them.

He bought a Model T Ford touring car. He could not drive so he hired "Fish Davis" to drive him around. He would go to Columbia every third week to sell cowhides and buy supplies for the store. I went with him most every trip. He always took sardines and soda crackers to eat. The trip took all day. When I was about 9 or 10 years old I got the car stuck in the sandy road (Railroad Ave.). He was blind then and I told him my predicament. "He said, lead me to the car." He put his hands on the back bumper, picked the back end of the car up, and set it out of the sand. Then he went to the front of the car and picked it up out of the sand. He was a strong man.

My Grandmother Flaherty was a seamstress. I never remember her using a pattern. Ladies would bring cloth in the morning and pick up their dresses in the afternoon.

My Grandfather, Tom Watson, got caught on a fence and could not turn loose of the broken electric lines. He was an early resident of Blaney, a farmer and merchant. He was married four times.

One of the first doctors to locate in Blaney was Dr. Grigsby. Before him the doctors would come from Lugoff, Ridgeway, and Blythewood. Dr. Grigsby's house and office still stand.

In May 1900, Jesse T. Ross became postmaster. He served until 1946. His wife, Georgia., filled in until 1947. Then J. D. Watson, Sr. (my father) was appointed in October 1947. In August 1965, I was appointed postmaster and served until May 1987. In 1980 the post office served about 1100 families. When I retired in 1987 we were serving 3300 families. (Note--After 1881, the Pendleton Civil Service Act required that postmasters and mail carriers pass civil service examinations before being appointed.)

They built the Blaney School Gymnasium in the late 40s and had only $20,000 to use. I was a teacher during that time at the school and made $3200 per year. The school had a football team and a basketball team with an outside court."

Some early residents of Blaney:
Butler Evans.............**Hot Dog Stand**
A. T. Simpson...........**Hardware Store**
Jack Bailey...............**Fertilizer, Feed and Seed**
Warren Sanders.........**Farmer, Grocery Store**
Arlin Rose................**Gas Station and Garage**
Walter Rose..............**Toll Collector Wateree Bridge**
Bookman Family........**Grits Mill and played fiddle**
Goff Family..............**Grocery Store**
Henry Ross...............**Farmer and Merchant**

The Art of Discrimination...

The assassination of President John F. Kennedy in November 1963 was the catalyst for the passage of the Civil Rights Act of 1964. President Lyndon B. Johnson made a speech before the Congress of the United States on November 27, 1963, in which he said that no memorial could better honor the fallen president than the passage of the civil rights bill on which President Kennedy had worked so hard. President Kennedy had called for the passage of the bill on June 11, 1963. It was not easy on the House or the Senate, but the bill finally passed muster, and President Johnson signed it into law on July 2, 1964.

This piece of legislation was a milestone in American history and would change forever interactions between African Americans and whites, males and females, and government and people. The bill outlawed all major forms of discrimination against racial, ethnic, national and religious minorities, and women. It ended unequal application of voter registration requirements and racial segregation in schools, at the workplace, and by facilities that serve the public. But its enforcement requirements were weak, and many roads would be traveled on the way to true equality.

It was 1965 before the first steps to integrate Kershaw County schools were noticeable. Supt. Arthur Stokes announced, "All students in the county public schools will have freedom of choice to attend any school in the county, regardless of race, color or national origin." Twenty-nine African American student applicants were assigned to white schools by May of 1965. No white students applied to African American schools.

In the summer, Project Head Start, a biracial kindergarten program for the disadvantaged, was started. In the fall, three schools, Bethune, Blaney, and Camden were desegregated using the freedom-of-choice plan.

In August 1967, the commissioner of education advised Supt. Stokes that the county freedom-of-choice plan was not working. The county was declared "not in compliance" with the Civil Rights Act of 1964, and all federal funds ($700,000 annually) would be withheld until compliance was achieved. Supt. Stokes began immediately forming a plan to completely desegregate all county schools.

Home Town Maintenance...

Blaney Mayor J. Don Watson, Jr. and Council set the town tax levy at 14 mills and mailed a notice to town residents in September 1964. The levy was to be used to pay for a new town hall building, fire truck, and other town expenses. A resolution had been passed on Sept. 8 to build a town hall on Ross St. with a $5,500 loan from SC National Bank. E&S Construction of Cayce got the bid for construction. Town meetings were to be held in the basement of Blaney Baptist Church during the town hall construction. In November, the council requested that the county delegation approve two-year election terms for town officials instead of one.

In 1965, the new town hall was completed, and town officials moved in on January 12. New furniture included desks, chairs, table and chairs for council meetings, and two dozen folding chairs. A call to community men to form a volunteer fire department was made with good response. A new fire alarm system was put into place using a two-party telephone system stationed at Potters Store. A Town Barbecue fund raiser was held on July 4th featuring 10 hogs, 10-12 pots of hash, and 50 chickens. With adults plates at $1.25 and children's plates at 75 cents, $700.81 was raised for town expenses.

1965 Elgin Town Hall

In 1967, the town bought its first typewriter. An ordinance was adopted to charge a $100 fine or 30 days on the county chain gang for false fire alarms. Contracts were let for paving rights on Elgin Streets. A caution traffic light was installed at the main intersection of Main and Church Streets in town. A resolution was adopted to transfer $5000 to the Bank of Orangeburg in Lugoff for a Gross Revenue Fund with a one-year savings certificate @ 4 ¾ percent interest. A resolution was adopted to expand town water lines constructed by developers to furnish water to subdivisions using 6" pipe for fire protection. The lines were to be deeded to the town in exchange for water.

New water rates were adopted--first 3000 gal. $3.50 minimum, next 7000 gal. 75 cents, next 15,000 gal. 60 cents gal., next 25,000 gal. 50 cents gal., and all over 50,000 gal. @ 35 cents per gallon.

In 1970, the town drilled three more water wells.   Virginia Well & Pump of Atlanta did the work on J. D. Watson, Sr's. land.

County Connections…

 A greatly improved telephone connection for long distance direct dialing was installed in 1963. Postal rates of 6 cents for a first class stamp and 10 cents for airmail also went into effect. In 1968, for the first time 25 women were selected for county jury duty. Also dedication ceremonies opened new dual lanes from DuPont over the newly named Howard F. Speaks (Wateree) Bridge on Hwy. #1   Feeder lanes were widened to accommodate 10,800 vehicles (75-80% local traffic) crossing the river each day. In 1971, the A. Sam Karesh Long Term Care Center with 88 beds opened within the Kershaw County Hospital premises to service the increasing elderly and disabled county residents. In 1969, John Conder opened Central Carolina Livestock Market off Hwy. 601 in Lugoff. It could handle 3000 cattle and some horses on sale day.

An Unpopular War…

President Lyndon B. Johnson called his administration's goals "The Great Society Program". Right away the civil rights legislation of 1964 was adopted followed by the Voting Rights Act of 1965. Medicare and Medicaid quickly came into being, and the federal food stamp program was created to improve nutrition and strengthen agriculture. More was coming to alter the "fabric of the nation's life" when war again loomed its ugly head.

  The Cold War-era military conflict involving North and South Vietnam, Laos, and Cambodia lasted from November 1, 1955 to April 30, 1975. The United States became involved in 1960 in an attempt to prevent communist takeover of South Vietnam. The American people, however, never approved of the war, and in 1968, as the war escalated, made their disapproval very clear to President Johnson. By the end of his presidency we were beginning to withdraw troops and seriously questioning General William Childs Westmoreland's tactics in this apparently unwinnable war. Gen. Westmoreland was from Spartanburg, South Carolina, and from 1964 to l968 was the Commanding General of U. S. Combat Forces in Vietnam. Col. Gregory Daddis, on staff at the U. S. Military Academy, said that "Westmoreland knew that success or failure depended on a political solution as well as a military one. And most important was that we have a stable government in South Vietnam which never materialized. You couldn't divorce one from the other." Four star General Westmoreland fought in three wars (World War II, Korea and Vietnam) for four presidents and was made Army Chief of Staff in 1968 by President Johnson. At the height of the war, 543,00 men were on the ground, and by the end of the conflict 58,220 American soldiers were killed. Gen. Westmoreland retired in 1972 and came back to South Carolina. He died in 2005 at the age of 91.

President Johnson decided he would not run for a second term. Kershaw County counted 15 war dead. John Larry Jeffers (age 19) of Elgin was one of the casualties. He was killed in action July 25, 1967, in South Vietnam, and one of our roads (Larry Jeffers Road) is named in his honor. An American Legion Post was also named in his honor, the Larry Jeffers American Legion Post 195 of Lugoff-Elgin.

Veterans returning home from Vietnam were not accorded the usual homecoming fanfare. With no parades or banners, just coming home, one by one, just like they left, with resulting psychological and drug problems for years to come. The mixed responses to our involvement in Vietnam added a new wrinkle to our national war times history.

Humpty Dumpty Had A Great Fall…

Richard Milhous Nixon was a good man who served his country well for eight years as President Dwight D. Eisenhower's Vice President. His first term as President of the United States, 1969-1973, went so well he was re-elected in 1974 with a landslide vote by the people. Everyone, it seemed, had nothing but good things to say about Richard Nixon.

His visit to China in 1972 opened up diplomatic relations with this vast, powerful country. Closely following this visit the détente and treaty he and his Secretary of State Henry Kissinger negotiated with the Soviet Union in 1972 gave us hope that this world power nation would no longer be a threat. In 1973, the Paris Peace Accords finally ended the Vietnam war. On the domestic front new wage and price controls were imposed, and social security benefits were enacted. Eighteen-year-olds got the vote, and the war on cancer and drugs was accelerated. The Environmental Protection Agency was established, and space exploration was scaled back. And then came his second term. His Vice President, Spiro Agnew, resigned in disgrace. Gerald "Jerry" Rudolph Ford, Jr. was the first person appointed to the vice presidency under the terms of the 25th Amendment, after Spiro Agnew had resigned. The Watergate scandal exploded as if a bomb had gone off in the country with wiretapping, charges and counter charges, and misconduct right and left, and by August 9, 1974, we saw on television a stranger who looked like Richard Nixon become the only president ever to resign. He resigned rather than be impeached and removed from office.

The entire spectacle, played out on our television screens for months, left a very bad taste in our mouths and a distrust for government that has been hard to forget. As a country we lost more than a president we trusted and admired, for we saw our country in disgrace and, in the end, we did not like what we saw.

When Gerald Ford replaced Richard Nixon as president one of his first acts was to pardon Richard Nixon. Ford's presidential pardon of Nixon was very controversial, and the country really never forgave him. During Gerald Ford's tenure, the country endured the worst economy since the Great Depression, with high inflation, and a recession. His subsequent loss to Jimmy Carter in the 1976 presidential election has come to be seen as an honorable sacrifice he made for the nation.

Georgertown Deep Sea Fishing Trip for Channel Bass Fish - Blaney Men
L-R, Back Row
Leroy Brown ,Vernon Nettles, Lonnie Moak, Alvin Spencer, Roger Ellisor, George Ross, Herman
Brazell and Charlie Wooten
L-R Fron Row
Alvin Kelly, Afon Strickland, Lemuel Wooten, J. R. Hornsby and Sam Watts
Courtesy of Lem Wooten

 **XIII**

Truth has no special time of its own
Its hour is now...always.
---Albert Schweitzer

Vibrations of Progress

United We Stand......

The Unitary School System began in the fall of 1970. The shakeup that resulted in the increase of students in certain schools involved consolidating, renaming, and doing whatever else was needed to accommodate and insure that all African American and Caucasian students in each attendance area attended the same school. In Blaney that meant a new building in Lugoff housing all Blaney and Lugoff high school students into Lugoff-Elgin High and Wateree School in Lugoff schooling Lugoff-Elgin middle school students. The school bus system became one system for all students instead of two systems. Teachers were assigned according to the ratio of black to white in the whole district. Problems? There were many, but everyone involved worked hard to make things work, and, in time, they did.

On Feb. 26, 1971, Charlie Wray Wooten was installed as Mayor of Elgin. Council voted to install street signs in town and agreed on names for streets. Some names chosen were Main, Church, Rose, Ross, Branham, Kelly, Bowen, Pine, Dogwood, and Watson Streets, Railroad Ave., Cherry and Surrey Lanes, Forest Dr., Smyrna, Blaney, Sessions, Green Hill, and White Pond Roads. Donald D. Carr was appointed as Town Police Chief and Fire Chief. A telephone was installed in Town Hall, and Leila Ross became Town Clerk.

In 1973, the first woman was elected to Elgin Town Council, Eva Bowen.

A garbage collection contract was given to H. T. Hornsby at $200 monthly for weekly pickups starting April 1. An easement was granted by the Kershaw County School Board in the northwest corner of county school property fronting Hwy. #1 for the purpose of building a new Town Hall.

This was the property on which Blaney High School was burned in 1956. Plans were approved for the new structure, and the low bid of $20,675, submitted by L. W. Wooten Construction Co., was accepted in October 1973. Financing included a $12,000 interest-bearing loan. The county health dept. was given the green light to hold weekly health clinics in the town hall. An annexation petition of the area adjacent to town on the southeast side of 75% or more residents was approved. Charlie Emanuel was hired as a water meter reader and town watchman.

1973 Town Hall

In 1974, town limits signs were approved for all main roads leading into town. Annexation on the north-by-north side of the Elgin detour running west to Smyrna Rd. was approved. A request was made to the county delegation to extend terms of office to four years for mayor and council with council seats staggered for two seats every two years for continuity. Twin bridges were erected over the Wateree River on the I-20 Interstate Highway marking a landmark road travel improvement.

A three member Election Commission was appointed in 1974 to plan and supervise town elections with Eva Garnes, Francis James, and Ray Strickland. A Zoning Commission was established to zone town residential and commercial areas, to review requests for new buildings, repairs, renovations of old buildings, and to approve all building permits. James Suggs, L. W. Wooten, and Bobby Stockman were appointed.

On July 1, 1974, building permit fees were set, and the decision was made to assign house and street numbers to all property within the town.

Building Permit Fees:

$ 500-10,000...........5.00
10,001-25,000..........10.00
25,000-50,000..........15.00
50,000-100,000......... 25.00
100,000-500,000...... 100.00
500,000-Up............ 200.00

February 4, 1975 elected officials sworn in were Charlie Wooten, Mayor, with Council Members Eva Bowen, Paul Grooms, Francis James, and James Suggs. Officer W. R. Sturkie was hired as Police Chief.

On July 15, 1975, Eva Garnes became Town Clerk. On August 26, 1975, Jackie Starling replaced Mrs. Garnes as Town Clerk. On October 10, 1975, Camille Burney became Town Clerk. On November 10, 1975, George Maxwell was hired as Town Clerk and Treasurer.

Mr. Maxwell was promoted to Town Administrator on Sept. 27, 1976. An article appearing in the *Camden Chronicle* upon his promotion stated that "George M. Maxwell, a native of Pulasky, Virginia, attended public school in Pulasky and upon high school graduation enlisted in the U. S. Army and received basic training at Fort Jackson, S.C. A veteran of Vietnam, Mr. Maxwell received the Combat Infantry Badge, the Bronze Star with two oak leaf clusters, the Purple Heart and the Good Conduct Medal. He is currently attending the University of South Carolina majoring in accounting and is to receive his B. S. degree in May 1977. He is an active member of the Elgin Lions Club and the Veterans of Foreign Wars."

Mr. Maxwell was relieved of his duties on a charge of embezzlement on October 10, 1977, and the town accepted a check from him in the amount of $2100. An audit of town books on December 12, 1977, revealed $8488.14 missing or unaccounted for in town funds. Mr. Maxwell was uncooperative and refused to answer a registered letter sent to him from the town. The town turned the case over to Royall lawyers on Jan. 9, 1978, and on May 16, 1978, Mr. Maxwell offered the town $5000 to settle and the town accepted.

An annexation petition was received from Jeffers Place on January 5, 1976. The town adopted the strong mayor council form of government on April 5 and voted to have a Catfish Stew Day in Elgin on December 4, 1976 (motion by Francis "Pete" James). A public meeting on September 21 to plan activities for the Catfish Stew Day included a decision as to the name for the annual festival. Sonny Smith suggested the name "Catfish Stomp." And everyone said, "Let it be done, let it be so."

The Catfish Stomp…

The Town of Salley had a hit on their hands in their annual "Chitlin' Strut". It drew thousands of people every year who just had to have a fried chitlin' and lots of money was made for various town projects. "Pete" James, an Elgin councilman, wanted to find "something" that would put our town "on the map", you know, "a destination place" where you could get something good to eat and have a good time, too. If the Town of Salley could do it, Elgin could, too. And so the idea of an annual "first Saturday in December" festival to be called "The Catfish Stomp" was born when the community put their heads together and dreamed "big".

The ingredients for the "stew" were no secret: Catfish (lots of it), Irish potatoes, onions, fatback, tomato base, and Texas Pete. The trick is in knowing how much, when to add, how long to cook, and finding the right chef to "put it all together". In the 36 years Elgin has had a Catfish Stomp we have had many chefs, but the first one was Ross Boulware who had a real talent for "putting it all together" and establishing that unique taste that people come back for every year.

Another essential for the festival is the annual Christmas Parade which actually started one year before the "Stomp" began. Jim Suggs was the first director of the parade, and Madge Strickland joined him in 1976 for the first "Stomp" Christmas Parade.

A carnival is another essential of the Stomp, and it usually stays in town for at least the weekend. Beauty pageants and "Womanless Weddings" are also entertainment folks look forward to every year. Over the years various events take place like the AAU Junior Olympic six-mile run, Lugoff-Elgin Band concerts, Patterson School of Dance exhibitions, car shows, arts and crafts displays, parachute jumps, gospel music, and clog dancing. Various celebrities appear like Miss America, Kylene Barker, in the 1978 Stomp. The Stomp has truly become a tradition in the town, and the thousands who descend upon Elgin every first Saturday in December seem to want it to continue…forever.

In Town News…..

In 1977, Jim Suggs was named the first Municipal Judge. Council voted to install sidewalks in town, and Billy Miles was hired to read water meters.

Billy Miles was promoted to Water Dept. head in 1978. The Elgin Water System had 517 customers. B. P. Barber and Associates (civil engineers) were asked to map and color code the entire water system. Open house for the new Fire Dept. addition to the Town Hall building was held July 16, 1978, and Miss America was the featured attraction at the annual Catfish Stomp in December 1978. The town paid her $500 for her appearance. A new flag pole was donated to Town Hall by the Elgin Lions Club.

On August 15, 1979, there was another change for the former Elgin Watch Plant property. Engineered Products Group took over the plant to produce V-belts. E. Reed Reynolds was manager.

The Day That Elgin Cried …

It was a beautiful sunny day, unusually warm for the winter day of February 21, 1974. Kershaw County Deputy Ernest C. (Chris) Potter III, at age 23, was assigned court duty in Camden. It was Court Day and prisoners had to be transported back and forth to the courthouse for court action on their cases. Chris was happy to do this job or any other that had to do with law enforcement. He was new on the job having been hired by Sheriff Hector DeBruhl just four months earlier (October 31, 1973), and he was eagerly anticipating going to the Police Academy for training in the profession he had chosen.

He had attended Georgia Southern University and worked at DuPont for a time, then he had talked to his dad about joining the sheriff's department, and his dad had given his blessing. He admired his dad, Ernest C. Potter Jr., who had been a marine in World War II, Mayor of Elgin in the 60s, a mailman and a fireman, and owned a grocery store. Chris loved playing chess, liked television, motorcycles, his 1963 Chevy Impala Convertible, and working in Potter's Grocery when he was growing up. He had a brother, Johnny, and a sister, Pattie, and he loved his mom, Gladys Goff Potter, who was not as keen as his dad on his being a deputy but always wanted him to be the best at whatever he did. She worked as Town Clerk when his Dad was Mayor, worked for Southern Bell Telephone in Columbia and was the switchboard operator at the Sandhill Experiment Station, but her main focus was her family. Chris had married his high school sweetheart, Jeannie Rose, and was looking forward to being a dad himself in about six months.

Deputy J. C. Tollison (age 32) received a call while at the courthouse from the sheriff's dispatcher that three men were thumbing for a ride on the I-20 Interstate near the Elgin exit. Chris asked Tollison if he could ride along and Tollison agreed. They did not know that the men were wanted for murdering a 59-year old Columbia man, C. Elmer Joyner, the night before and the murder of a Forest Acres Police Officer, Richey O. Finch (25 years old), earlier that morning. Law Enforcement Officers did not have the luxury of instant communication through cell phones, computers, and other devices like they would have today.

When they arrived at I-20 they saw only two men walking east on the interstate, and they circled around and parked the patrol car just past the Elgin exit near a guardrail. They both got out of the car. Tollison told Chris to stay by the car, and he walked over to the two men beside the road. He asked Theodore Byrd and Dennis Wilson for identification and asked that they step to the patrol car. Then he heard something and, whirling around, he turned to see the missing third man with a gun to Chris's head. McKinley Thomas had been hiding behind the guardrail when they parked.

Then Tollison felt a punch in his side. It was a gun held by Theodore Byrd. Dennis Wilson came over, put another gun to his head, and took his .357 Magnum service revolver away. Thomas had already taken Chris's .357 Magnum. The three hitchhikers now had five guns in their hands. They ordered the two deputies to walk down the road embankment side by side with their arms outstretched holding hands. Chris was on Tollison's right as they took a few steps and, at a nod to each other, broke into a run. All three men, Byrd, Wilson, and Thomas began shooting.

Tollison was struck twice in the head as he ran, and then he fell. He attempted to get up and was shot twice more. Chris took six shots that killed him as he ran and then fell, face down. They lay close to each other. Tollison waited until he was sure their attackers had gone and then struggled, and despite a bullet riddled face, arm, and shoulder, was finally able to stand up. Not knowing Chris was dead, he went to him and told him to lie still, he was going for help.

Leroy Johnson was a trucker from Tyler, Texas, driving east on I-20 when he saw Deputy Tollison near his patrol car trying to flag him down. He pulled over and assisted Tollison to the car telling him he would drive him to the hospital. Tollison insisted he check on Chris, which he did. He gently laid his jacket over him and left him in the care of other drivers who had stopped by this time. Within an hour, an ambulance picked up Chris and delivered his body to Camden Hospital where Tollison was already in surgery.

While hospital personnel worked on Tollison, a massive manhunt was in progress. The Kershaw County Sheriff's Office, SLED, and the National Guard along with local Elgin men and Chris's best friend, Harold Brown, were searching a 10,000 acre area throughout the night and the next day with no success. Chris Potter's killers had vanished.

Jeannie Potter was told by a co-worker and friend of the tragedy at her job in a mortgage brokerage office in Columbia. Upon receiving the news, she fainted. Her sister, Roberta, was there when she revived and, together with her co-worker, Frances Yon, they drove back to Elgin.

At the Elgin exit a roadblock had been set up with law enforcement manning the roadblock. Upon learning that Jeannie was in the car, they gave an honor salute with hands over their hearts and escorted them to Jeannie's father's house.

Upon learning of the death of her son, Gladys Potter was heart-broken, but true to form, she reacted with a strong resolve to be the rock her young daughter, Patti and son, Johnny, could lean on in the tumultuous days ahead. His dad, E. C., Jr., was inconsolable.

A few days later, at the urging of his family, McKinley Thomas, 20 years old, surrendered. Then the names of his accomplices became known, and the manhunt intensified. Governor John C. West, a Kershaw County native, offered a $5000 reward. Ten days later, Dennis Wilson, age 19, turned himself in to Philadelphia, Pa., authorities. On March 12, 20 days after the incident, Theodore Byrd, 25 years old, walked into a Detroit, Michigan, police station and gave himself up. Sheriff DeBruhl and SLED Chief J. P. Strom returned Byrd to South Carolina.

Chris Potter's funeral on Sunday, February 24, was eulogized at Highway Pentecostal Holiness Church with approximately 1200 in attendance. The burial was held at Hillcrest Baptist Church in Elgin. The burial service was delayed until the long cortege of cars could reach the church and park. The two churches are only one and a half miles apart. Chris's favorite 23rd Psalm was read at his funeral, and he was buried in his deputy's uniform.

Byrd pleaded guilty and claimed he was the only shooter. He was sentenced to life in prison for murder, 20 years for shooting Tollison, two consecutive 25 year sentences for armed robbery, 10 and 5 years consecutively for grand larceny and breaking into an auto, and 30 days for carrying a concealed weapon. Thomas and Wilson were tried together in their June 1974 Columbia jury trial, pled innocent, and were exonerated of the murder. They were found guilty and sentenced to 20 years for armed robbery and one year for carrying concealed weapons to be served concurrently.

Justice was swift in 1974. Byrd pled guilty just three months after being brought back to South Carolina. Thomas and Wilson got a change of venue and a joint trial. Byrd, star witness at the Thomas/Wilson trial, claimed he was the only shooter despite testimony that three guns were used. These judgments were rendered at a time when the death penalty was not in force in South Carolina. The death penalty was reinstated in South Carolina in 1985 after a people's campaign petition with over 15,000 signatures.

E. C. Potter IV, "Little Chris", was born six months after his father was killed. He is now a Sgt. in the Richland County Sheriff's Office.

Chris's best friend, Harold Brown worked for the Kershaw County Sheriff's office before becoming Chief of Police in Elgin in October 1993.

At this writing, Theodore Byrd at 64 years of age is in the Broad River Correctional Prison. He was later convicted of the murder of Forest Acres Policeman Richey O. Finch and is serving concurrent life sentences for the murders of Chris and Finch. He comes up for parole every two years. Jeannie Potter has attended every parole hearing since he began serving his sentences.

J. C. Tollison served as a Kershaw County Deputy for another 23 years, retiring in 1994. He served in the Elgin Police Department for two years beginning on July 1, 1995.

Jeannie Potter has never remarried. She works for the Speaker of the South Carolina House of Representatives, Bobby Harrell, as his Executive Assistant.

In the early 90s, the Kershaw County Sheriff's Office and the Town of Elgin dedicated Potter Law Enforcement Center on US Hwy. #1 and Ross Street in honor of Chris and his father, E. C. Potter, Jr. "Little Chris" was given "Big Chris's" deputy badge.

In May 2013 an additional honor came to the Potter Family. The property facing the home of Ernest Christian Potter, Jr. on Potter Dr., located on the corner of Green Hill Road and Main Street in Elgin, was named Potter Community Park by the Elgin Town Council. The property owned by the Town of Elgin has been used in the last few years for the annual Catfish Stomp and the Podunk Festival.

National Scene...

Jimmy Carter from Georgia was elected President of the United States in 1976 with a 53% voter turnout, the lowest presidential voter turnout on record.

The country was in the wake of the Vietnam and Watergate fallout and soured on government at that time. President Carter did not adapt well to Washington ways and culture though he tried very hard to emulate President Roosevelt's fireside chats, wearing his sweater and urging Americans to save energy by cutting off lights and lowering thermostats. Gas rationing did not add to his popularity, and in 1979 when Iran took 50 American hostages and an April 1980 rescue mission failed, America had had enough. Jimmy Carter became a one term president.

2012 Blaney Fire Department

 XIV

Climb Every Sand Hill

The Great Communicator...

Ronald Reagan was elected President of the United States in 1980, and within the first hour of his presidency the American hostages in Iran were released. The former movie actor got the votes of 44 states and pledged to restore America's reputation in the world and respect here at home. In 1981 he quickly became known as a champion of conservatism and "the Great Communicator". On March 30 an attempted assassination left him with a punctured lung and the admiration of a nation which badly needed a hero. Peace through strength was the cry as he re-established American power abroad and initiated more military spending. Confrontations included the Grenada attack and the Soviet Empire show-down. In 1987 the Iran-Contra affair prompted an apology to America, and a scandal was averted. The peaceful end of the Cold War and a visit in 1988 to the Soviet Union restored faith in government and the presidency. He finished up eight years in the White House as the Berlin Wall crumbled.

Camden Journal-Elgin Response...

May 22, 1879 "We are at a loss, for there is nothing to report. Those who are not sick are well, those who are not dead are alive, and those who are not married are trying to be."

Well, actually there were a few notable moments in Elgin history in the 80s. Dr. Robert A. Cochran retired as town physician after 30 years of good and faithful service. The Elgin water system had growing pains with more subdivisions being built to accommodate the "bedroom community" population of those that worked in Columbia and Richland County and wanted a nice quiet town to come home to after a hectic day "in the big city". Billy Miles was offered the job of manager of the water system and given a raise in salary. He reported that the pumping station was inadequate and we needed a new well. Bill Nelson was hired for part-time work with the water dept., and L. W. Wooten Construction agreed to train Nelson on installing new water taps.

A Recreation Commission was created on June 10,1980 with nine members, Paul Grooms, Mr. Tarte, Willie Dixie, Peggy Wilke, Don Miller, Bert Mauldin, Earline Hall, Barbara Dorton, and Pat Goff. And the town found it necessary to establish a Planning and Zoning Commission on August 12, 1980 with seven members: Loretta Carr, Roger Ross, John Powell, John Murray, Carol Neese, Dick Yandle and Melvin Elders.

Walmart came in 1980 and caused a boom of chain-type stores to follow. The "superstore" built near the Wateree River became "the place" to buy groceries and anything else you needed (almost). Fast food eating places began to appear on both sides of Elgin (Columbia and Camden), and residents liked being in "the middle" of shopping centers galore.

The interstate highways saved a lot of time going to work or shopping to Columbia and beyond, and newer/better automobiles and trucks allowed environmental "comfort" with radios for entertainment.

Subdivisions built from the 1960s into the 21st century surrounded Elgin and enlarged the infrastructure needs and voting power of the area. Some subdivision names are: Tall Pines, Blaney Hills, Haigs Creek, White Hills, Jeffers Place, Baldwin Place, Rosewalk, Whippoorwill Farms, Elgin Estates, Stratford Plantation, Windy Hills, Smithfield, Cobblestone, Bradford Village, Hunters Crossing, Sandwood, Aberdeen, Wedgewood, Elgin Acres, Quail Creek, Thunderwood, East Point, Brentwood, Pine Forest, Pine Mark, Needle Point, Four Seasons, Laurel Crossing, Taylor Oaks, Wind Mill Ridge, Wood Trace, Kelsey Ridge, Brookside, Laurel Ridge, Sandy Creek, and Saddlebrook.

1981 brought new council members, Loretta Carr and Marshall Danenberg, and a new town clerk, Nettie Campbell. James Suggs was mayor. Paul Grooms became the new fire chief on June 16. Council passed a motion to prohibit the town from doing business with any person who is a town official. This applied to immediate family members of town officials and also to companies in which they have a substantial business interest. Exceptions were permissible after review and approval by council. John Wells became town attorney on October 20. In November Luther G. Dyson became police chief.

A new industry in the form of Westvaco Corp. started up in September 1982 as a part of a $7 million expansion by the company in South Carolina. The new Elgin chip mill produced wood chips for pulp and paper for rail transport to Charleston.

Mayor Francis "Pete" James and council members Loretta Carr, Mike Gilchrist, Bryce Smith, and Roger Ross had a "hot potato" handed to them in a council meeting in October 1983. A resident, Jeanette Quinn told the council that she had 80 signatures asking that the town of about 500 be dissolved because "Elgin was pasted on the front page every time you pick up a newspaper," and "if residents have to hold the council's hands, why even have a town council?" That issue and several others were discussed in the 90 minute council session. In addition to some council members, John Wells, town attorney and Paul Grooms, fire chief made comments discouraging the action. Various votes were made by council over the course of several meetings in October and November. The first was to have a referendum to dissolve the town, then to rescind the referendum ordinance to dissolve the town and/or recall council members. Finally an ordinance opposing dissolving the town was passed after two readings on January 9, 1984. Paul Grooms was elected to council on March 19, 1984 replacing Mike Gilchrist who had resigned from council on November 30, 1983.

Ground breaking ceremonies for the new Elgin Cablevision Office in August 1984 signaled the beginning of three months of construction work to service up to 700 homes. The cable system would offer 21 channels with a 54-channel capacity. On hand for the ground breaking were Mrs. Ernest Amburgey and Cullen Amburgey, co-owners; Elgin Mayor Pete James; Peggy Wilke, town employee; Bryce Smith, town council member; and Linda King, Kershaw County Chamber of Commerce.

Regular election for two council seats on Feb. 12, 1985, saw Bryce Smith and Jim Wheaton sworn in as council members. Roger Ross resigned on May 14, 1985, with special election on

May 21 electing Frank W. Thompson as a council member. Hillcrest Baptist church was annexed into the town limits, and it was announced that the proposed Elgin Neighborhood Park had received funding for the project.

Economic downturns usually happen slowly enough that you are alerted early on that changes might be on the way. The area's largest employer, DuPont, began layoffs in the mid-1980s followed by changing work schedules indicating downsizing was taking place. In 1986, employees were being offered "early-out" packages urging retirements, and many took advantage of the opportunity to either go on to other employment or "go fishing". For the time being, DuPont continued their role as the industrial impact leader in the county.

HBD Thermoid Company (HBD Industries) came to town in 1986 and set up shop in the former Watch Plant on US Hwy. #1 at the edge of the town limits. The company, which was founded in 1914, produces industrial and specialty hoses, conveyor belts, V-belts, timing belts, and PT belts. Plant Manager Michael Craven is the current chief executive of the plant which has successfully operated in Elgin for 27 years.

The Elgin Pharmacy opened in April of 1986 and partners Freddie Mubarck and Tony Casey embarked on a 27-year (so far) journey serving Elgin citizens with their pharmaceutical needs. Tony relates that he and Freddie had discussed opening a pharmacy for years but the tipping point was when the First Citizens Bank opened in Elgin in 1985, and Mayor Pete James remarked that the only thing folks in Elgin wanted more than a bank was a drugstore. They then looked into a Bruce Sloan building that was under construction and bought up a North Carolina pharmacy's stock in a bankruptcy sale and the "rest is history". Their business today is "bursting at the seams", but Tony says expansion will be "left to the young people" of tomorrow.

In November 1985, the First Citizens Bank opened in temporary quarters at the old Blaney Drug Store across from Town Hall to applause from the whole town but especially Mayor James who had worked "real hard" to attract a bank for the growing town. Citizens rushed to open accounts, and Mayor James wanted to be first, but had to settle for second when Roger Ross beat him to the punch.

Photos Courtesy of First Citizens Bank and Anna Chason

In March 1986, the bank moved into larger new quarters on Main Street, and the dedication was one to be remembered. Hammy's Bar-B-Que cooked and served barbecue for the whole town in the Blaney School Gym across the street from the bank. Bank Manager Bob Woods initiated the official grand opening by cutting a ribbon of dollar bills which were donated to the Elgin Benevolent Fund accepted by the President of the Fund, Rev. Bill Coates, Pastor of Blaney Baptist Church. Mayor Francis "Pete" James voiced his welcome to the new First Citizens branch and everyone enjoyed the Blue Grass Band music played for the special occasion.

Blaney Elementary School was built on Smyrna Road in Elgin in 1985 by Martin Engineering, Inc. with architects Wilkins-Wood Associates. The general construction cost was $2,900,000 with 70,000 sq. ft. It opened in 1986, and the Dedication Ceremony was held April 26, 1987. Robert Falls was county superintendent and Carl Robinson was the first principal of the school. Faculty and staff included 34 teachers, 2 secretaries, 4 custodians, 3 aides, 8 food service workers, 1 nurse, and 1 psychologist. Rose Sheheen was principal for many years and Lisa Carter is the current principal of the school.

1985 Blaney Elementary School
Photo by Judy Darby-Buchanan

Jeffers Place, Best Looking Street Award

Rose Sheheen and Madge Strickland 1992
Catfish Stomp Check presented to Blaney School

Loretta Carr was elected (the first woman) mayor in 1987 with Bruce Sloan, Margie Howard, Paul Grooms and Bryce Smith on council. The Jeffers Place subdivision was annexed in 1987. In 1989 the East Point subdivision and village was annexed.

Hurricane Hugo...

It began on September 9, 1989, just off the coast of Africa but grew into a Category 5 hurricane passing through the Leeward Islands and giving a glancing blow to Puerto Rico before heading out to sea where it calmed somewhat into a Category 2 hurricane. But when it felt the warmer waters of the Gulf stream, it again strengthened just before hitting the South Carolina coast, now a Category 4 hurricane.

Folks on the coast had prepared for a Cat. 2 hurricane and were surprised to be facing sustained winds of 140 mph and a storm surge of 18 feet at landfall in McClellanville, South Carolina, northeast of Charleston. With sustained winds of 137 mph and gusts of 160 mph plus a 30 mph forward movement, it arrived in the inland town of Elgin around 2 AM.

As many residents hunkered down in the safest part of their homes, the winds howled and whined and whistled around and around in a seemingly endless pattern until all of a sudden the frightening noise stopped. The eye of the storm had arrived. Many went out into the night of terrors to "see what they could see". Many trees were uprooted, cars and trucks tossed about, and an eerie silence soon gave way to an increase in wind speed and a quick dash back into shelter for the second half of the nightmare.

The early morning dawn of September 22, 1989, was relatively quiet except for the whine of chain saws cutting up the trees that were blocking every street and road in town. Blaney Baptist Church's steeple had toppled, power lines were down everywhere, parts of buildings and roof pieces covered the ground, but there were no reports of fatalities in or around Elgin, a minor miracle to say the least. Local wind gauges registered 100 mph or more but only 2 inches of rain.

The power was slow to come back on with many people without electricity for a week with food spoiled in freezers and ice hard to come by. Damage claims to insurance companies were numerous and settlements slow due to the volume of claims filed. Debris removal was a problem and went on for weeks. Kershaw County was declared a disaster area. After coming inland near Charleston the storm moved on to North Carolina, Virginia, West Virginia and Ohio, winding up a remnant low near Lake Erie. Some statistics on the (Sept. 9-25,1989) hurricane reveal that 61 fatalities were recorded (27 in S. C.) and the highest wind was 162 mph. The number of people left homeless topped 100,000, and some people were without electricity for 18 days. There was $7 billion in damage in the United States and Puerto Rico.

The Blaney School Gymnasium, built in 1949, fell victim to the vicious storm. Inspection of the building revealed that it was structurally unsafe, and it was demolished by the School District in the early 1990s.

Special mention should be given to these first responders who made all the difference in meeting this emergency in the Elgin Community:
Fire Chief Allen Robinson, Police Chief Dennis McKelvey, Water Dept. Mgr. Billy Miles, and Kershaw County Sheriff Hector DeBruhl.

Chapter XV

*Some men see things as they are
and say Why?
I dream of things that never were
and say Why Not?
--George Bernard Shaw*

Water Without Wells

"Bush 41", as he came to be known after his son was later elevated to the Presidency of the United States, was elected in 1990 and served only one term because the people could not forget his broken campaign promise of "no new taxes" as he was forced because of the economy and the politics of the time to "raise taxes". But George H. W. Bush was a good president and commander in chief during the Iraq invasion of Kwait and the resulting "Gulf War".

The 1991 town elections were held on February 5. Francis "Pete" James was elected mayor, and Madge B. Strickland and Paul Grooms were elected to council to serve with Roger Ross and John Storemski. On October 16 a new "black beauty" fire truck was the pride of Fire Chief David Bagwell. On December 10 Matt Lynch was appointed Zoning Administrator.

The publication of the first Elgin Town Newsletter was approved by Council on April 4,1991, with Madge Strickland serving as editor. It was not mailed out due to postage costs but made available at town hall for all who were interested.

Amtrak Train Derailment…

In the early morning of July 31, 1991, possibly the worst railroad accident in South Carolina's history occurred in the swamps behind DuPont's May Plant. Enroute from Florida to Washington, D. C. on an 18-car Amtrak train, 426 passengers were jolted awake when, all of a sudden, the train swiped two empty CSX cars on a side rail after its rear cars jumped track. Authorities blamed the 5:00 AM accident on a defective switching device which ultimately caused the loss of eight lives and caused about 100 passengers to be injured. The DuPont Emergency Response Team and Fire Brigade personnel rushed to the scene and worked with other first EMS responders to care for and transport the injured to hospitals in Camden and Columbia.

Darkness and the location of the accident made rescue efforts more difficult. Passengers who were not injured were cared for by the Red Cross at Camden High School which was converted into a temporary emergency shelter by school personnel. Volunteers set up cots and tried to attend to the needs of the stranded passengers. Local restaurants provided food and drink.

Three "Welcome to Elgin" signs were erected in 1992 at the three main town entrances. Kelly Johnson became the new police chief on March 17. John Wells was hired as the town attorney on July 14.

Water Crisis…

It began with a water quality report on July 24, 1992, from the South Carolina Department of Health and Environmental Control (DHEC) that Elgin Well #5 did not meet the United States EPA Maximum Containment Level standards for safe drinking water due to the presence of tetrachloroethylene in the well water. The town council convened in an emergency session, and, after learning that public health could be in danger, decided to send out a public notice, investigate treatment options, and look into alternate sources of water with a unanimous vote.

The Council further learned that tetrachloroethylene was a toxic colorless organic liquid with mild chloroform-like odor with the greatest use in the textile industry and in aerosol dry cleaning products.

The National EPA and South Carolina DHEC are charged with promoting and protecting the health of the public and the environment as directed by the 1974 Safe Drinking Water Act passed by the Congress of the United States. They have set Maximum Containment Levels for tetrachloroethylene at 0.005 milligrams per liter or 5ppb with a goal of ZERO. Potential negative health effects are increased risk of cancer and problems with the liver.

Within 18 days Billy Miles, Water Dept. Mgr. was granted $1000 to process a test well, asked to check out financing for a new well, secure a new well site and put out bids for the well. He was also given instructions to blow off Well #5 with DHEC permission.

DHEC reported on September 8, 1992, that the town had two contaminated wells (#5 and #8) with trichloroethylene and tetrachloroethylene present and that they were trying to find the source but that the source might never be found, which was not an uncommon problem. DHEC stated the town had done everything possible to protect the customers from using the contaminated sources of water (the wells had been shut down). Miles reported he had found a new well site and was waiting for necessary approvals from land owners and others.

Council was advised that trichloroethylene was a known carcinogen and dry cleaning solvent (chlorinated hydrocarbon used as an industrial solvent, a clear, non-flammable liquid with a sweet smell). The Maximum Containment Level was 5ppb, and the greatest use was as a degreaser for metal parts. Trichloroethylene can cause central nervous system depression and possible heart defects.

On September 14, Council met with Lugoff Water District officials to offer a proposal which included rates and a contract to possibly purchase wholesale water from them. Miles had a telephone quote from Columbia Water Dept. on the purchase of bulk water.

On September 21, Council held a workshop to discuss alternate ways of bringing water to Elgin. On October 13, Council voted to proceed with a 12" water line from Lugoff to Elgin. On November 4 Council met with the Lugoff Water District. Council proposed to agree in principal to merge the two water systems, to have BP Barber Engineers conduct a study of cost analysis and engineering feasibility with Elgin paying 1/3 of the study costs, and to have John Wells research legal requirements for a merger. The record would include a possible referendum of the people in Elgin. With two members of council absent, the vote was in favor by the three council members present.

December 8 John Wells advised that a referendum on the water merger would be necessary and a 6-week notice was required. A decision was made to have Wells write the referendum/ordinance question and submit it to the McNair law firm for approval. The December 15 first reading of Ordinance #131 proposing the merger with Lugoff Water District was in favor. The second reading of the ordinance on December 22 was also approved by council.

On February 2, 1993, the town referendum vote was 95 for the merger and 87 against. On February 9, with the Lugoff Water District officials present, John Wells introduced Ordinance #133 ratifying the election on Feb. 2 and setting forth the format for the merger. The main concern was to satisfy FHA and the bonding attorneys so that the new water department could issue bonds to meet future needs. A motion was made to call the new department the "Lugoff-Elgin Water Authority". The motion carried. On Feb. 16, Ordinance #133's first reading passed. An amendment to Ord. #133 failed to pass. On Feb. 23 Ordinance #133's second reading to merge Lugoff and Elgin water departments passed. An amendment to the ordinance failed to pass.

A new council member was elected on February 2, 1993. Joseph I. Romer, who would take office in March. John Storemeski was re-elected. They would join with Madge Strickland and Paul Grooms to form the 1993-94 council with Mayor Francis "Pete" James still in office.

On March 9, 1993, Mayor James stated the water merger had been signed with Lugoff, and Don Watson and Roger Ross had been appointed to the Board of Directors for Elgin. Paul Grooms introduced Ordinance #134 to repeal the merger. A Special Meeting of Council was called to further consider on March 15. First Reading of Ord. #134 on March 15 to amend Ord. #133 to include the Elgin Council in negotiation with the Lugoff Water District passed. The Second Reading of Ord. #134 on March 22 passed.

On July 20, John Wells reported that the Lugoff Bond Attorney had sent him a letter saying the closing of the merger would be Tuesday, July 27. Wells brought information on the merger on July 24 that the value of the Elgin Water Dept. had been estimated by Billy Miles to be $2 Million. Council motioned that Lugoff must sign assumption of Elgin obligations and change the name to Lugoff-Elgin Water Authority before deeds would be signed. The vote was unanimous.

The merger between the Lugoff Water District and the Elgin Water Department was finalized on July 27, 1993. Water lines had yet to be run between Lugoff and Elgin.

The foregoing record of council deliberations during the water crisis is a chronicle of the facts involved. But the issue goes deeper than mere facts and figures. The Elgin Water Department came into being in 1962-63 when the Elgin Watch Company came to town and the town decided to change its name to Elgin. Changing the name of the town was a divisive issue that just would not die a natural death. Added to that was the struggle the town went through emotionally and financially to get a water system up and running efficiently. With that

Photo by Anna Chason

accomplished and with the great number of families moving into the Elgin community needing plentiful, safe water, in the intervening 30 years, the water department became a point of pride in what the town could do and continue to do. The hometown water department death sentence that DHEC delivered in 1992 was not believed or accepted by about half of the town and the town council. Half wanted to maintain the "status quo" and hope for the best while the other half were not willing to gamble the health of its citizens and the lack of adequate water for current and future needs. The Lugoff Water District was the first to draw drinking water from Lake Wateree and build a treatment plant in 1974. Their quality and quantity of surface drinking water was excellent, and the management was professional. Today the Lugoff-Elgin Water Authority has been merged successfully for over 20 years providing excellent quality and quantity service to the thousands of customers who live and thrive in the Elgin and Lugoff water district.

Back To The Basics...

Madge Strickland, Chairman of the Catfish Stomp Festival, presented a check for $318 on March 9 to Boy Scout Troop #318 for tents, backpacks, and sleeping bags. Another check was given to the Elgin Police Department for $6,500 for a car video camera and recorder. These amounts were part of the profit from the December 1992 Catfish Stomp Festival.

New Police Chief H. Harold Brown entered service for the town of Elgin on October 13, 1993. Police Chief Kelly Johnson had resigned on July 30. An auxiliary police officer, J. C. Tollison, was hired to assist Chief Brown on July 1, 1995. He stayed two years before retiring.

Old Blaney School Property...

After the Blaney Graded and High School burned in 1956 it was replaced with another school in 1958 on property owned by the Kershaw County School Board in the middle of the town of Elgin located just behind the burned school property on which the Elgin Town Hall had been built. In 1972 the high school moved to Lugoff into a new Lugoff-Elgin High School building and the middle school children moved to newly renovated Wateree Middle School. In 1986 the grammar school children moved into a new Blaney Elementary School on Smyrna Road in Elgin. This left the school buildings in the middle of the town vacant, and in time they began to deteriorate and were vandalized. Townspeople frequently complained that the property should be put to some good use since it was a temptation to vagrants and a constant eyesore as well.

Eight years went by before an offer came to Elgin Town Council from the Kershaw County School Board on February 8, 1994 to give the town three acres of the old school property in exchange for the town re-zoning 8.53 acres commercial. The Elgin Zoning Board recommended that the town not accept the offer but to refer the offer back to the school board to consider an alternative plan and report back to council.

On March 8, the Elgin Zoning Board met to work on re-zoning the school property. On April 12, Mike Van Brunt, Zoning Chairman, discussed with town council a letter received on March 4 from Linda Scoggins, a White Hills subdivision resident, regarding rezoning the school property. Council voted to decline the February 8 school board offer and proposed an alternative preferred by the Zoning Board: "Request that the school board transfer the entire property to the town. The town would rezone the front 2-3 acres general commercial. The proceeds of the property sale would be used to raze or renovate portions of the old school building complex. The bulk of property then could be leased to the County Recreation Department for athletic fields, etc. Local government agencies, humanitarian groups, civic organizations, etc. could then lease or rent portions of the buildings."

Another ten years went by with no documentation in town council records of any official action taken. On July 19, 2004, the school board began tearing down the old school buildings. On September 28, rezoning of six-plus acres on the backside of the old school property from general residential to downtown commercial was proposed in town council meeting. First Reading was approved. On October 12 the Second Reading was also approved.

Today, Elgin Town Hall, newly renovated in 2012, occupies the front corner of the property. Businesses now on the property include a large Food Lion Grocery Store, the Old South Restaurant, Elgin Veterinary Hospital, City Laundry and Cleaners, Spoiled Rotten Beauty Shop, Subway Foods, Circee Nail Spa, Panda Garden Restaurant, Domino's Pizza, San Jose Mexican Restaurant, Dirty Laundry-Coin Laundromat, Art Werx Hair Studio, Embroidery Stitches Plus, Island Tanning, Better Body Fitness, Sunset Spirits, H&R Block, Advance America Cash Advance, and Auto Zone.

A Dream Come True...

For years in Blaney-Elgin, parents, teachers, politicians, and readers of all ages dreamed of the day when they could go to their own local library for books, research, private reading, and computer time.

The legacy of Mrs. Charlotte Theresa Snyder and her husband, Anthony T. Snyder, enabled the reality of that dream. Mrs. Snyder was raised in Germany and met her soldier husband during World War II. After the war they moved to Columbia and finally settled in Elgin. From the time her husband became an invalid until his passing, Charlotte devoted herself to his care, her dogs, and her garden, but her greatest joy was found in books. She was an avid reader and found a whole new world was open to her, and she never had to leave home. Her home was full of books, and, as Charlotte's own life drew to an end, she strongly desired to share the excitement of reading with others. Having no children of her own, Charlotte wanted to leave a legacy to the people of Elgin, and so her final wish was that her home on its 3-acre site should be used for a library.

The deed to Mrs. Snyder's property was transferred to the Town of Elgin on August 17, 1993. Mrs. Snyder willed her home and property located beside U. S. Highway #1 in Elgin to the town of Elgin to be used as a library. On June 14, 1994, town council looked at the property with the view toward clean-up of the grounds and renovation of the house to be used as a town library. Council decided the property could be used for a library and made plans to set up a "Friends of the Library" fund for donation of money and books to help with expenses. They noted there was a garden on the property that could be restored.

On August 8, 1994, Council voted to renovate the Snyder building if possible into a library. They proposed getting bids from a contractor for feasibility and cost and discussed setting up a fund to defray the construction cost.

Two years later on September 10, 1996, an ordinance was drafted to set up funds for an Elgin Community Library. On December 10, council agreed to give use of the Snyder land valued at $90,000 to the Library Fund and agreed to maintain the building after the library was built. Council voted to give $20,000 per year for three years, a total of $60,000, to the Library Fund.

On September 9, 1997, General Obligation bonds were approved by council for the library. The architectural contract for the library was awarded to Curt Davis and Associates on July 16, 1997.

The John T. Stevens Foundation gave $10,000 to the library on January 13, 1998. The construction contract for the 3637 sq. ft. library was awarded on March 10, 1998, to Mike Hilliard Construction Co. of Heath Springs, S. C. at the low bid of $348,888.

The new Elgin Branch Library operating under the auspices of the Kershaw County Library was dedicated on Sunday, June 6, 1999. State Representative William F. Coty was the speaker for the occasion.

The agreement between the Town of Elgin and the Kershaw County Library Board under the direction of Frances M. Whealton was renewed November 13, 2001, stating that the Library Board would provide all books, equipment, and staff and pay all telephone and computer costs. The Town agreed to retain ownership of the building and furnishings and to provide water, electric, and alarm system services. The Town would also make necessary repairs to the interior and exterior of the building and maintain the grounds. The branch library would remain under the supervision of the Kershaw County Library Director.

In August 2009, Amy Schofield, Director of the Kershaw County Library, met with Elgin Town Council and advised that the Elgin Library had outgrown the current location and needed remodeling or perhaps a move to Lugoff.

Elgin Branch Library

Library ribbon cutting with Paul and Viola Grooms

Mayor Pete James advised the Library Board on February 19, 2010 that the Town of Elgin wanted the library to remain in Elgin and offered 4.22 acres in town on the Main @ Greenhill Rd. location for a new branch library and would give an annual contribution of $18,000 for operating expenses.

Today the Elgin Branch Library continues to operate in "tight" but adequate facilities. The county funds for building a new library did not materialize when the sales tax referendum failed in 2010.

Elgin Town Council approved in May 2013 the naming of "Grooms Garden" in honor of Viola Grooms, wife of the late Mayor Paul Grooms. Mrs. Grooms faithfully tended the gardens surrounding the Elgin Branch Library.

Charlotte's dream became our reality; her legacy of knowledge, hope and love continues.

Meanwhile...

There was a 1994 movement within the county to replace the old garbage littered roadside trash dumpsters with fenced in recycling centers that would accept household garbage, newspapers, plastic containers, beverage bottles, used oil, yard trash, junk, white goods (appliances), and possibly glass and many other items. The recycling centers would operate under the supervision of county employees and would be open at certain times and every day but Sunday and Wednesday. The public was notified by newspapers and notices that the old dumpsters would no longer be in use after the opening of the recycling centers.

HBD Thermoid Co. of Elgin (HBD Industries, Inc.), formerly B. F. Goodrich Co., which occupies the former Watch Plant site, leased to the county the necessary land for the Elgin Recycle Center on November 8, 1994. The recycling center opened on February 25, 1995, with a ribbon cutting ceremony, music, prizes, and entertainment. For the past 18 years, the center has been a resounding success and continues to operate under county management.

Two resignations of note at Town Hall were Mayor Francis "Pete" James(resignation June 10, 1994) to accept the job of West Wateree Magistrate, and Madge Strickland who resigned October 11, 1994, from the Town Council to serve on the Lugoff-Elgin Water Authority Board.

In a special election held on September 6, 1994, Paul Grooms ran for mayor unopposed and was elected.   Two newly elected council members were sworn in on February 14, 1995, Norman A. Ernst and Walter D. Coleman.   Judy Darby-Buchanan was hired as town clerk on April 12, 1995.   An ordinance to increase the town tax rate from 27 to 28 mills was approved in 1995 by council.

The 1995 Kershaw County Council Seat #3, vacated by Hammy Moak, was filled by John Wells, local attorney, who ran for the seat unopposed.

The town mourned the untimely passing of Fire Chief Thomas Jaye Buff who was killed on interstate I-20 on November 14, 1995. A Lake City policeman was returning to Florence County after attending Police Academy training in Columbia when his vehicle struck Chief Buff. The Blaney Fire Department had responded to a call on the interstate from a vehicle accident. An elderly couple were sideswiped on the other side of the highway, and Chief Buff had walked over to them to offer assistance. His son, Thomas Buff, is now serving as a volunteer firefighter on the Blaney Fire Department.

The first town annexation in 8 years occurred January 9, 1996, when Windy Hills subdivision became a part of the town. In March 1996, the Kershaw County Chamber of Commerce reported to Council that Elgin had been selected as one of the top 50 places to live in the United States according to the April 1996 issue of Money Magazine.

A new police "Policy and Procedures" manual by Chief Harold Brown was approved by the Police Academy and adopted by the town council on January 14, 1997. A new Fire Chief, Terri Kearns, began February 11. Joe Romer and John Storemski were re-elected to council. Dr. Ralph Cain, Kershaw County Supt. Of Education, announced in March that construction of a new elementary school for the Elgin area had been approved due to the increase in school population. A new Asst. Municipal Judge, Chuck Chavis, was appointed in April. A Public Hearing at Town Hall introduced the Municipal budget for the 1997-98 Fiscal Year on June 2, 1997 with $186,475 projected revenue and expenses at 27 mills tax rate. Walter Coleman resigned from Council in July since he had moved out of the town limits. Todd McDonald replaced Coleman in a special election November 11, 1997.

A change in the Lugoff-Elgin Water Authority merger contract was made in February 1998 to make the contract a one year renewable agreement to allow for changes and flexibility annually.

The new Leslie Stover Elementary School ground breaking ceremony was held May 17, 1998, and the new school built to accommodate the rapidly growing Elgin school population opened on Smyrna Road in Elgin in August 1999. Present for the dedication of the school on October 17, 1999, were Governor Jim Hodges and State Supt. Of Education Inez Tennenbaum. Principal Glenn Huggins reported that for the School Year 1999-2000 the student population at Blaney Elementary was 725, and the school population at Stover Elementary was 833.

Stover School groundbreaking 1998
Courtesy of Jimmie Rose

Photo by Judy Darby-Buchanan

The DuPont company in Lugoff made major facilities improvements in 1998, and the community was surprised to learn that they had sold the plant to another chemical company, Invista, Inc. (Koch Industries) in 2003. Invista continued the DuPont tradition of being the county's largest industrial employer with 800 employees by 2008.

The February 1999 town elections continued Paul Grooms as mayor with Norman Ernst, William L. Salter, Jr., Don Williams and Anthony T. Pope on council. On January 12, 1999, Doug Coleman was appointed Administrative Judge for the town assisting Judge Bill Hyman. In December 1999, the Catfish Stomp Festival celebrated its 25th Anniversary with approximately 10,000 people attending the 3-day festival which included a beauty pageant, parade, catfish stew, carnival, exhibits, and other special events.

Sewer System...

Elgin's growing population, business increases and the addition of a new elementary school necessitated serious consideration by the county in February 1999 to run sewer lines into town along Hwy. #1 and across to the new school on Smyrna Road.

By January 2003 additional plans considered were that the sewer system would come into Elgin on Main Street (US Hwy. #1), turn left at the Main St. and Church St. traffic light intersection and then go down White Pond Road to the frontage road at the I-20 interstate. This would accommodate a proposed business park and medical center.

On November 30, 2004 the Elgin Town Council voted to pay $360,000 from the General Fund to Tom Brigman, contractor, for four town sewer projects with Kershaw County bringing the sewer trunk line in by the end of February 2005. Mayor Paul Grooms and council approved Ordinance #187 to grant the county a 30-year non-exclusive franchise and consent for provision of county operated sewer service dating from February 15, 2005. Easements were granted on June 14, 2005, by Sarah Emanuel, Mike Taylor, Gayle & Roger Ross, Franklin Nelson, Tyler Baldwin, and Dennis Arledge.

After a delay in construction of the sewer line, there was a restart in August 2005 to finish the project. In October 2006 the county returned $14,840 to the town which was the balance of money not used on the sewer line of the original $360,000 the town had invested in the project with the county.

As expected, the installation of the sewer line has been an economic boon to the town business development, and the cooperative venture between Kershaw County and the Town of Elgin has been beneficial to all concerned. The success of the project can be traced specifically to the diligent efforts of County Administrator Bobby Boland, Nelson Lindsay of the Kershaw County Economic Development Office, and C. R. Miles, Kershaw County Council, as well as, the Elgin Mayor and Town Council.

In 1999, a newly renovated concrete bridge was re-opened across the Wateree River between Camden and West Wateree. The bridge was christened the Bobby T. Jones Bridge named for the South Carolina Department of Transportation Commissioner (a Kershaw County native). The new bridge enabled north and south traffic to again flow on side-by-side separate bridges greatly reducing traffic tie-ups and accidents. This was a good note on which to end a century and begin another.

1962 Post Office.
Courtesy of Jean Watson

1985 Post Office
Photo by Dusty Rhodes

PORTRAIT PROFILE

Daughter of
Ella Branham Coker and John Coker
Wife of Arlin Rose
7/27/1937 -

CHILDREN
Donna 1955
Becky 1963
GRANDCHILDREN
Jonathan 1978
GREAT-GRANDCHILDREN
Gabe 2007
Caleb 2010

JIMMIE DILLARD ROSE
5/3/1938 -

>Jimmie Rose was born in Blaney, S.C.
>1956 Graduate of Blaney High School
>1957 -1991 - Secretary in Blaney Elementary School
>1993 - 2002 - Kershaw County School Board Member
>Member of Highway Pentecostal Holiness Church, Elgin, S.C.

  Except for a brief stint at the Mental Health Clinic in Columbia, Jimmie Rose has devoted her life to elementary school education in Blaney, S. C., serving over 40 years in the Blaney Schools and on the Kershaw County Board of Education. She is retired now living on the Sweet Air Horse Farm near Elgin, S. C., with her husband, Arlin, enjoying the fruits of her labors. Children whose lives she has touched number in the hundreds, and many still contact her for that "touch of kindness".

Chapter XVI

Sail fast, Sail fast,
Ark of my Hopes, Ark of my Dreams;
Sweep lordly o'er the drowned Past,
Fly glittering through the sun's strong beams;
Sail fast, Sail fast,
Breaths of new buds from off some drying lea
With news about the Future scent the sea...
--Sidney Lanier, Baltimore 1878

Two Thousand and Counting

The State of the Nation...

The economic health of the nation during the Bill Clinton presidential years (1993-2001) is undeniable, yet, as his presidency waned and scandals arose, Americans found that more and more the media and the internet gained prominence as an adversarial court of opinion. Things were not black or white, but gray as the people tried to sort out who were the good guys versus the bad guys. Two thirds of the American people said the impeachment trial of Bill Clinton was harmful to the country and that the country was morally on the wrong track. Many felt that whatever the state of the economy or world affairs, honesty, integrity, and good moral character are necessary to the office of the presidency. Independent Council Ken Starr, with the permission of U.S. Attorney General Janet Reno, spent $70 million in his investigation of the Clinton scandals and leaked lurid descriptions of presidential sexual encounters to the press and posted to the internet. In 1998, the U. S. House of Representatives impeached Clinton on two charges, perjury and obstruction of justice. He was acquitted in the US Senate in 1999 by a margin of 17 votes. He was only the second president to be impeached in the history of the United States. Andrew Johnson was the first who was also acquitted in the Senate by a margin of 1 vote. Our 42nd president is remembered for a very positive job performance but negative personal behavior in office.

George W. Bush defeated Al Gore (Clinton's Vice President) for the presidency in 2001 in a grueling, long, drawn-out ballot count that involved the Supreme Court before he was declared the winner of the electoral vote. Bush would be sorely tested within eight months of his oath of office by a terrorist attack on our native soil.

9/11...

Four coordinated terrorist attacks were unleashed upon New York City and Washington, D. C., by the Islamic terrorist group al-Qaeda on September 11, 2001. Four passenger airlines were hijacked by nineteen al-Qaeda terrorists to be flown into buildings in suicide missions.

American Airlines Flight 11 and United Airlines Flight 175 crashed into the north and south towers of the World Trade Center in New York City. It took about two hours for the towers to collapse, and much damage was also done to ten nearby buildings. American Flight 77 crashed into the west side of the Pentagon in Washington, D. C., damaging the headquarters of the U. S. Defense Department. United Flight 93 targeted the US Capitol building but crashed into a field near Shanksville, Pa., when the passengers stormed the captain's cabin.

Three thousand people died that day including 227 passengers and 19 hijackers on planes. Osama bin Laden, al-Qaeda leader, claimed responsibility in 2004 and was killed in May 2011 by US Forces. He claimed the motive was U. S. support of Israel, U. S. troops in Saudi Arabia, and sanctions against Iraq among other issues he had with America.

The United States launched a "War on Terror" and invaded Afghanistan to depose the Taliban which had harbored al-Qaeda. The 9/11 attacks led indirectly to the wars in Afghanistan and Iraq as well as additional homeland security with the cost totaling at least 5 trillion dollars. The Department of Homeland Security was created, and the USA Patriot Act was passed by Congress. The FAA assigned sky marshals, and the Aviation and Transportation Security Act created a federal force to inspect passengers and luggage causing travel delays and personal privacy issues. By the end of Bush's two terms in office there were no further terrorist attacks, but there was a 1.2 trillion national budget deficit.

Significant effects were felt in the national economy and global markets. An immediate cultural impact saw a greater focus on family and home life, higher church attendance, and increased patriotism.

The 2008 presidential campaign resulted in the election of President Barack Obama, the first African American president. Double-digit unemployment gripped the nation as thousands of citizens lost their homes. Congressional gridlock threatened to paralyze the governmental processes as severe political tactics took hold in working out the balance of power between the President and Congress. The Affordable Health Care Act was passed in President Obama's first term and was a "bone of contention" in the 2012 elections with Obama winning a second term handily. The Congressional Budget office reported a 2012 federal budget deficit of $1.1 trillion.

Time and Tide…

9/11 changed our world forever, but even before that tremendous changes were going on in Elgin and really all of West Wateree. The population had nearly doubled within the last decade, and new technology surrounded us as the digital world captivated us with personal cell phones, laptop computers, hand-held computers, itunes, iphones, apps, ebooks, downloading of songs and movies, and all sorts of other "gadgets" that threatened to turn us into solitary communicators who avoided the personal contact with others our ancestors had always done. Everyone had a personal automotive vehicle with the freedom and income to expand their horizons beyond local living areas. Confidence in government was rapidly eroding, and illegal immigration employment was growing in the local labor and service areas as natural born Americans pursued better educations and better jobs.

In Elgin two more housing developments were annexed into town, Brentwood (1999) and Pine Forest (2002), and the town began accepting the state 1% sales tax revenue (2001) which offset the previous 27 mill town tax. C. R. Miles Construction Co. completed a U. S. Hwy. #1 project to create a center turning lane from Surrey Lane to Bowen Street in March 2002. In June, a school resource officer was assigned to Stover Middle School through a grant given to the Elgin Police Department.

Elgin Postmaster Barry Alter reported in October of 2004 that Elgin had 10 mail routes and was adding a new mail route every 6-8 months and making adjustments in mail routes with a lot of growth being seen in the Elgin area.

Judy Brock, Kershaw County Election Commissioner, reported to town council on January 8, 2008, that Elgin was increasing in numbers of voting precincts from two to five. They were Elgin Precinct #1 voting at Blaney Baptist Church, Elgin Precinct #2 voting at Blaney Elementary School, Elgin Precinct #3 voting at Elgin Town Hall, Elgin Precinct #4 voting at Stover Middle School, and Elgin Precinct #5 voting at Harmony Baptist Church. This change was necessary due to the increase in numbers of registered voters in the Elgin area and in order to be in compliance with state law on the numbers of registered voters assigned to each polling place. This change was approved by the County Legislative Delegation and the SC Election Commission. Since that time, due to the large number of voters assigned to the Elgin Precinct #3, another voting precinct has been approved. Elgin Precinct #6, at the new Blaney Fire Department on US Hwy #1, was used for the General Election in November 2012. In January 2009 the town council passed an ordinance on an agreement with the Kershaw County Election Commission to handle all municipal elections for the town in the future using SC Election Commission rules and regulations.

Paul Grooms retired in 2007 after serving the town continuously as council member, fire chief and mayor for 31 years. He began on council in 1975 for a 4-yr. term. He was the fire chief from 1979-1984. He again served on council from 1985-1994 when he was elected mayor. He was mayor from 1994-2007.

Pete James retired in 2011 after serving the town for 18 years. He served as a council member for two terms and mayor from 1983-87, 1991-94, and 2007-11. Judy Darby-Buchanan retired in June 2013 after serving the town for 18 years as town clerk and clerk of court (1995-2013). Nettie Campbell retired as town clerk in 1995 after serving the town for 14 years (1981-1995).

Judge W. R. (Bill) Hyman died in office in 2010 after serving as the chief municipal judge for Elgin for 23 years (1987-2010).

Local newspaper publications began to appear starting with "*The Elgin News*" with Fred Davidson as editor, which was granted a town business license in December 2004. The *West Wateree Chronicle*, a weekly full service newspaper was on the streets in April 2008.

A highlight for Elgin was the start-up of a big supermarket, Food Lion, in the middle of the town in September 2005. Dollar General appeared in February 2005. The annexation of 28 acres for Chaise Builders at the corner of Watson and Bowen Streets in March 2007 created excitement as the builders proposed 44 patio homes and 23 single family homes on 67 lots. First Citizens Bank of Elgin celebrated 25 years as "The Bank of Elgin" in 2009. The bank was a success from the day it opened in 1985 in temporary quarters, moving into their present facilities in 1986.

Town Hall Growing Pains…

In November 2002, the council purchased the Wooten property on the corner of Main Street (US Hwy #1) and Greenhill Road for $140,543 with the intent to build a new town hall on the property. On May 13, 2003, council approved having an appraisal done on the present town hall. A decision to advertise for an architect to begin a plan and design for a new town hall was made in August 2004. Council selected James Stewart, architect, on July 12, 2005, to design the new town hall. A contract with him was done in September 2005. A topographical map of the Greenhill Rd. property was done by Riddick and Associates for $3850 in October 2005.

Jim Stewart, architect, presented drawings for the new town hall and fire department on July 11, 2006. In December 2006, a tentative ground breaking date was set for January 5, 2007, at 11:00 AM.

In 2007, there was a lot of interest in buying the present town hall. In October 2008, a low bid of $1,030,423 was accepted from Randolph & Sons for construction of the new town hall. Two bids were received for the present town hall in January 2009, $105,000 from Dennis Arledge and $65,000 from Mary Ward.

On January 23, 2009, the mayor and council discovered a statement on the last page of the town hall deed, "that should the property described cease to be used for public purposes by grantee, possession thereof and title shall revert to the School District of Kershaw County". Council immediately rejected the bids on the sale of the present town hall, declined the bond issue on the new town hall, and declined the construction contract on the new town hall.

On March 3, 2009, C. R. Miles, the Elgin representative on Kershaw County Council, announced that a new 5000 sq. ft. county Blaney Fire Department would be built on US Hwy. #1 next to the Recycling Center with three bays, and living quarters upstairs. Council discussed the need to remodel the present town hall and called in a consultant.

In January 2012, Mayor Brad Hanley presented a $102,680 contract issued to Chaise Builders, General Contractor, for remodeling the old fire department space in town hall. He announced that Chaise would be using all Elgin labor and subcontractors. Council members Norman Ernst, Melissa Emmons, Roger Ross, and Larry Risvold voted unanimously to proceed.

Asbestos removal necessary in the town hall renovation cost $6975 and took three days to remove. Council approved this on March 16, 2012.

The remodeled Elgin Town Hall Dedication and Open House was held Thursday, September 6, 2012, with Mayor Brad Hanley presiding. Prayers were offered by Rev. Ken Jackson of Hillcrest Baptist Church and Rev. Phillip Blankenship of Blaney Baptist Church. Speakers were John Wells, Attorney; Police Chief Harold Brown, Town Council; Judge David Reuwer; Judge Dennis Arledge; and State Representative Laurie Slade-Funderburk. The tour of the facility included the new police headquarters suite, council chambers/court room and town clerk office and town hall lobby. Refreshments were served. Judy Darby Buccanan, the town clerk, acted as hostess for the event which was well attended by the town residents and guests.

Police Commendations...

Cpl. Shannon Cook of the Elgin Police Department received the Medal of Valor, the second highest award to any police officer, in June of 2003. He assisted Kershaw County Deputy Richburg with a mental patient who had set a mobile home on fire. Cook talked the patient out of committing suicide.

Elgin Police Chief Harold Brown was voted into the American Police Hall of Fame and Museum in Titusville, Florida, for his 30 years of service and effective law enforcement, and community involvement and improvement. It was an honor well deserved. Richard DeVors, a longtime friend, former Elgin police officer, and colleague, presented the award on January 8, 2008 at the Elgin Town Hall.

The ranks of the Elgin Police Department employed in 2013 to protect and assist Elgin citizens include:

Chief Harold Brown,
Photo by Judy Darby-Buchanan

Chief Harold Brown
Doug Barton
Lt. Alan Wilson
Leslie Corey
Lt. Ed Hines
Dennis Vincent
Sgt. Renee T. Wilson
James Fitzgerald

Elgin's first drug dog, "Hunter", retired October 3, 2007. Two K-9 dogs are in Elgin law enforcement service in 2013.

The "Podunk" Festival was first observed in Elgin in 2011 and was the brainchild of Police Chief Brown and his department to be a fundraiser for the annual Christmas Toy Roundup for children every December. It is a one-day event held in April in Potter Community Park on Greenhill Rd. and Main St. every year and features a parade, exhibits, food vendors, staged entertainment, and "Movies on Main" outdoor movies.

Caring Hands...

In the early 1900s, a hometown boy began his private practice of medicine in the newly organized town of Blaney. A Kershaw County native and graduate of Blaney schools, Leesville College, and the Medical College of Charleston, William Duncan Grigsby and his wife, Lillian Maud Burns, served the Blaney community for 42 years.

After the 1948 death of Dr. Grigsby, the community welcomed Dr. Robert Anderson Cochran in 1949 as he began his general practice of medicine in Blaney. He was a native of Pennsylvania, a graduate of Ursinus College and Temple University School of Medicine, and had just completed eight years of military service in the US Army. Dr. Cochran and his wife, Ruth Marie Brooks, served the Blaney-Elgin community for 34 years.

Together these two dedicated, beloved family doctors delivered hundreds of babies, treated thousands of medical maladies, administered shots, made rural house calls, bound up physical and emotional wounds, and even treated the "Blaney Wildcats" and occasional ailing livestock. Many times their services were paid for with poultry, garden vegetables, labor, and promises to pay later. Both of them also gave of their time and resources to local schools and to government and community events.

The only local hospital was Camden Hospital which opened in December 1913. This hospital moved to Roberts Street in Camden in 1958 and was renamed Kershaw County Memorial Hospital. This name was again changed in 1994 to Kershaw County Medical Center and finally to Kershaw Health in 2009. Expansions of Kershaw Health appeared in the county after the turn of the 21st century in Bethune, Lugoff, and Elgin. The new Elgin Outpatient Center opened in 2009 and offers Cardiology, Imaging, and Laboratory services. Five Kershaw Health Primary Care physicians are in practice there. The Elgin Urgent Care Center is housed in the same medical complex which is adjacent to the I-20 interstate highway at the Elgin Exit.

Elgin Outpatient Center,
Photo by Dusty Rhodes

I-20 interstate and US Hwy. #1 highways provide easy, time-saving access for Elgin citizens to Columbia and Lexington area doctors and hospitals which are used by many Elgin residents. Ambulance service is provided by county EMS units. Prior to 1967, emergency care ambulance service was furnished by funeral homes.

The Sentinel Health Partners office with resident physician Dr. Paula L. Belmar opened in Elgin in 2005 and moved into a new larger office in 2011 in order to accommodate the large numbers of patients in the area.

Public Service Interests…

In a special election in June 2004, the county's first female representative, Laurie Slade Funderburk, was elected to the SC House of Representatives to fill the unexpired term of Vincent Sheheen, who won a special election in February to fill the SC Senate seat vacated by the death of Senator Donald Holland who had held that office for thirty-three years.

The Elgin Town Council 2005 election brought Melissa Emmons to council to join John Storemski, Don Williams and Scott Jacobs.

Upon Don Williams resignation in March, Brad Hanley was elected to council. The 2007 election brought Francis "Pete" James back as mayor with council members Brad Hanley, Jerry Jeffers, Scott Jacobs, and John Storemski. The 2009 council election was won by Roger Ross and Larry Risvold.

The 2008 Kershaw County Council election for Seat #3 brought C. R. Miles representing Elgin to the council in Camden replacing John Wells who had served since 1995.

The 2011 town elections produced a new mayor, Brad Hanley, and returned Melissa Emmons and Norman Ernst to council. The 2013 council election was won by Edward Smith and Dana Sloan. A special council seat election in June 2013 to replace Norman Ernst (resignation) was won by Candace "Candy" Silvers from a field of four candidates.

Photo by Anna Chason

Hammy Moak, long-time county council member, also operated Hammy's BBQ Restaurant in Elgin which had become a state-wide attraction. Hammy closed the 39 year-old Elgin landmark on July 4, 2008.

Claude Campbell Store,
Photo by Anna Chason

Another well-known community gathering spot, Campbell's Grocery Store, closed October 13, 2007, after 61 years in business. The thriving store was operated by Claude Campbell and, until his untimely death, his father, Thomas Edward "Ed" Campbell. Ed Campbell had left the store the evening of June 12, 1982, and went home but did not show up the next day for a family Sunday dinner. He was found dead in his home, the victim of a robbery and assault.

The son of a family friend pled guilty to armed robbery and murder and is serving a prison life sentence. Claude Campbell says he kept the store open in part to honor his father, and also he felt obligated for all the many loyal customers they had served over the years. Campbell's Grocery opened in 1946 on U. S. Hwy. #1 (Main Street) in Blaney, and Claude began working there at age 23 in 1953. There were seven robberies at the store in 60 years, but closing it was never an option. It was commonly known that "if you didn't know the location of Claude's store, you're not from here".

Educational Encore...

As Kershaw County entered the 21st Century, there were three high schools, four middle schools and eleven elementary schools plus another middle school and one more elementary school on the drawing board.

The county employed 750 teachers and other school personnel making it the largest employer in the county. Ten thousand students (give or take a few) were being educated, not counting the students at the Continuous Learning Center, the Applied Technology Education Campus, and programs for adult education.

The Schools Timeline for Blaney-Elgin Students

1915   Blaney Grammar & High School in Blaney
1931   New brick 2-story Blaney Grammar & High School in Blaney
1949   New Blaney Gym in Blaney
1956   Blaney Grammar & High School destroyed by fire in Blaney
1958   New Blaney Grammar & High School in Blaney
1972   New Lugoff-Elgin High School in Lugoff
1972   Wateree Middle School in Lugoff
1986   New Blaney Elementary School in Elgin
1992   New Lugoff-Elgin High School in Lugoff
1992   Old L-E High School used for L-E Middle School in Lugoff
1999   New Leslie Stover Middle School in Elgin
2002   New Doby's Mill Elementary School in Lugoff
2008   New Lugoff-Elgin Middle School in Lugoff

Goff Feed and Tack, (Old Blaney Depot)
Photo by Judy Darby-Buchanan

Pine Grove School...

South Carolina's only residential facility for autistic children with severe mental or behavioral problems has come a long way since the Pine Grove School in Elgin was founded in 1970 with only five students. The school is located off US Highway #1 near Elgin on 40 acres of land, 15 miles north of Columbia.

Carl Henning, the founder, who retired in January 2007, says that the school was started before autism was discussed in polite company, and in the beginning there were so few residential programs for severely affected children, he thought he would start one, and it ended up working out. David S. Perhach, President, and James D. Moen, CEO, took over the school in 2007 and today operate the private special education school for special needs children offering four group homes. The capacity is about 35 students with over sixty staff members and many consultants. The students come from many different states and some from foreign countries.

PORTRAIT PROFILE

WILLIAM RALEIGH HYMAN
7/13/1937 - 4/22/2010

The son of
Hoyt and Mae Hyman
Kingstree, S.C. County of Williamsburg
The husband of
Valerie Miles

CHILDREN
Michael David Hyman - 11/12/1963
James Brian Hyman, Sr. - 12/30/1965

GRANDCHILDREN
Shannon Elizabeth - 12/31/1985
James Brian Jr. - 10/30/1989
Steven David Hyman - 10/21/1990
Jetson and Colby Woodland

GREAT GRANDCHILDREN
Kaylee Alexis - 8/23/2005
Landon D'Shawn Kirkland - 6/14/2011

>1953-1975 - Command Sergeant Major, U.S. Army
>Kershaw County Deputy & Wolfe Mechanical Purchasing Agent
>1987-2010 - Chief Municipal Judge, Town of Elgin, S.C.
>Member and Deacon of Blaney Baptist Church, Elgin, S.C.

Growing up in Williamsburg County in the Pee Dee Section of South Carolina, Bill Hyman was intrigued by the stories his four older brothers told about life in the military. He joined the army at age 16, just seven months before he reached the minimum eligible age. His military service carried him overseas to Korea, Okinawa, Germany and Vietnam where he saw combat action and earned the Combat Infantry Badge, Expert Infantry Badge, and Four Bronze Stars, (one for Valor) as well as the Air Medal, Purple Heart, Vietnam Cross of Gallantry with palm, Army Commendation Medal, Meritorious Service Medals, and numerous service medals.

He felt privileged and honored to serve the people of Elgin as their Municipal Judge for 23 years and also was a strong advocate for veterans. When not in court, he was the commander of the 130-member American Legion Post in Northeast Columbia.

He was a loving husband and a devoted father to his family. He is buried in Blaney Baptist Church Cemetery, Elgin, S. C.

Elgin Centennial Clock, Elgin S.C.

Chapter XVII

If Only we are Faithful to our Past,
We shall not have to fear our Future.
The cause of Peace, Justice and Liberty
Need not Fail and Must not Fail.
--John Foster Dulles

The American Dream

Blaney-Elgin 1908-2008…

The Town of Elgin was going to be 100 years old on January 23, 2008, and Mayor Francis "Pete" James, Police Chief Harold Brown, and the town council decided early in 2007 that the centennial year should be celebrated in a way that would honor the traditions and culture of the past as well as inspire seekers of "the American Dream" to hope for a better life than older lands and ages ever afforded. January 23, 2008, was designated as "Centennial Day", and the theme chosen was "History and Heritage".

On May 8, 2007, Shirley Stockman Miles, a 30-year retired US Veterans Administration Hospital Patient Representative, who just happened to also be a life-long resident of the community, accepted the town council appointment to be the chairperson of the Blaney-Elgin Centennial Committee. She began immediately to choose a board of directors who would assist in the planning and execution of this "once-in-a-lifetime" challenging occasion.

Cathy Brown was chosen as co-chairperson; Mayor James as committee advisor, Donnelle Stockman, secretary, Tabitha Keenan, treasurer; Renee Wilson, co-treasurer; and John Wells, legal counsel.

The board of directors crafted a missions statement for the centennial celebration - "Commemorate, Celebrate, and Educate the Citizens and Visitors on the History and Culture of Blaney-Elgin since 1908". They also agreed on a train as the Logo and a Motto, "Roaring Into The Future".

SubCommittees chosen were:
Advertising & Promotions ....Fred Davidson and Hillard Nelson
Beautification...........................Sharon and Jerry Jeffers
Business Contacts......................Gayle and Roger Ross, Linda Eyers and Teri Pruitt
Church Contacts........................Joyce Dyson
Entertainment...........................John Paul, Fred Davidson, Pam Delk, Hillard Nelson
Fund Raising ....Anna Chason, Sarah Pawlick, David & Lou Thomason
Grounds................................. Larry Tucker
Historic.................................Lou Thomason, Pat Goff, Fred Davidson, Nettie Campbell
                                      and Sonya Green
Town Mural............................Gayle Ross
Parade..................................Tana Simmons
Schools & Day Care Centers ....Sharon Gaudlitz
Security & Safety......................Police Chief Harold Brown
Vendors & Exhibitors.................Bill Miles and Sonny Goff

Goals to be attained were set and published.
1. The celebration would involve not just the Town of Elgin, but the
    entire Blaney-Elgin community with a 29045 Zip Code.
2. Commemoration of the history of Blaney-Elgin since it was
    chartered as a town in 1908.
3. Educate the community in the local history for the 12 months of 2008
    and forward.
4. Renovate the building donated for a museum and history center.
5. Establish and locate Monument Square as a town park.
6. Buy a 4-dial 15 foot town clock for display in Monument Square.
7. Sell engraved bricks to be displayed in Monument Square.
8. Sell time capsule space for concealment under town clock to be
    opened at the Bi-Centennial in 2108.
9. Paint a Town Mural on the oldest store building in Elgin.
    (The 1928 Warren Sanders store.)
10. Post Office will sell the official Centennial Cancellation stamp
    at $3 each in a collectible cover from January 23, 2008, to February
    22, 2008.

Planning for the major centennial festivities began in April 2007 and culminated with an October 14 joint meeting with the Kershaw County Historical Society at Hillcrest Baptist Church Fellowship Hall in Elgin. Panel Members were life-long Blaney-Elgin citizens who related their memories of the early days in Blaney. Larry Dixon made an audio/visual DVD of the meeting preserving the remembrances of Rev. Tommie Williams, Doris Maddox, Preston Goff, Virginia Monroe, Vernon Nettles, Bertha Goff, and Claude Campbell.

On December 1, the first vendor fund raiser took place at the annual Catfish Stomp Festival. In 2008 Kershaw County Councilman C. R. Miles presented the town with a $10,000 grant for Centennial expenses. Also, Sen. Joel Lourie presented a $5000 grant toward the town clock. The Centennial Committee raised $75,000 in grants and donations for the Centennial Celebration.

During the 2007 preparation the entire community was kept informed of the planned centennial activities by radio, town newsletter, *The Elgin News* , church announcements, and one-on-one contacts including the telephone. The excitement and anticipation gathered "steam", and the community participation and attendance at all events was "history making".

The Opening Ceremonies on January 26, 2008, were held in Stover Middle School with John Paul acting as Master of Ceremonies. Guest speakers were Mayor James, Senator Joel Lourie, and Representative Bill Coty with entertainment provided by Scott and Soupy Jacobs. The Elgin Idol contest, (first round) was enjoyed, and door prizes were given.

The second celebration event was on February 23, 2008, "A Tribute To Veterans" ceremony in the Blaney Baptist Church Gymnasium. The tribute began with the Pledge of Allegiance to the flag and a welcome by George Bozeman, Sr. Officer of Elgin VFW Post 11079. The Invocation was given by Charles Davis of American Legion Post 182, followed by a stirring rendition of the National Anthem by Madge Strickland. Winning essays and drawings by Elgin school children were presented, and awards were received by Caylin Watson and Kaycee Robinson of Blaney Elementary School for their drawings. Essay winners were chosen out of 66 essays written and were Savanna Gary, Destiny Ferrante, and Ashlyn Boyd of Stover Middle School. Mrs. Barbara Ray of the Kershaw County Veterans Affairs Dept. in Camden gave a short speech in which she said there were 5,814 veterans in the county in 2008 and that we had 49 killed in WWI, 98 killed in WWII with 24 prisoners of war, 12 killed in Korea, and 15 killed in Vietnam. Closing remarks were made by Shirley Miles, Chairperson of the Centennial Committee.

The next big centennial affair occurred on March 22, 2008, and really was two events in two places on the same day. The biggest and best ever Easter Egg Hunt sponsored by the Target Distribution Co. was held in the morning at Blaney Elementary School. Then in the afternoon at Blaney Baptist Church there was a "Festival of Choirs", welcomed by Jimmy Suggs. Pastor Phillip Blankenship gave the Invocation and the participants were Blaney Elementary School Chorus, Stover Middle School Chorus, Rehoboth Baptist Church Choir, Elgin Church of God Choir, Pontiac FBC Choir, and Hillcrest Baptist Church Choir.

VETERANS HONOR ROLL

Photo courtesy by Phyllis Nettles Martin

<u>Past Hero</u> - Vernon (Sarge) Nettles (August 30, 1918 - April 4, 2008)

A Kershaw County and Blaney-Elgin native, Vernon joined the US Army March 3, 1942, at Fort Jackson. He served during World War II in Tunisia, North Africa, Sicily, Normandy (D Day), North France, Rhineland, Ardennes, and the Central Europe Campaign. He was awarded the EAMET Campaign medal with seven Bronze Stars and various other medals. He was discharged Sept. 20, 1945, with 34 out of 42 months overseas time.

"He loved his country, a true veteran"…

Judge Bill Hyman

<u>Present Hero</u> - Joseph N. (Joe) Tate (July 7, 1948)

Born in Washington, D. C., now a true Elgin transplant, Joe joined the US Army on January 13, 1967, and served with distinction in Vietnam as a young 19-year old infantry unit medic. On December 16, 1967, he pulled three soldiers out of a burning armored personnel carrier (tank) which had been hit by a rocket-propelled grenade and put them on a helicopter for transport to field hospitals. Shortly after the incident his commander, John Theologos, recommended that Joe be given a Silver Star for his heroic actions. Joe ran into his old commander in 2008 at a service reunion, and he asked Joe if he had ever gotten his medal. Getting a negative reply, Col. Theologos resubmitted the paperwork, and just recently it was approved. Joe was discharged from the Army February 1, 1987, and had already received the Bronze Star. On May 1, 2013, forty-six years after the battlefield action, Joe received his long over-due Silver Star at the West Columbia National Guard Armory at a Vietnam Veterans celebration. The Silver Star is the third highest military decoration for valor that a soldier can receive and is given for distinguished gallantry in action against an enemy of the United States.

Photo courtesy by Joe Tate

The final centennial celebration, "Downtown Blaney", began with a 60+ unit parade down Main Street at 10:00 AM. Judy Gaston, a WIS-TV personality, was the lead-off parade marshal, and WPUB 102.7 reported the parade on live radio. Parade trophy winners were "Best Church Entry" - Smyrna Methodist Church, "Most Creative Entry" - Hillcrest Baptist Church, and "Best Overall Entry" - Elgin Red Hatters. Presentations followed, "Under the Big Tent", by Jennifer Miller, DJ, to parade participants, and oldest citizen contest winners, Eliza McCants, 94 years old, and Pearl Branham, 92 years old. Elgin Idol finalists performed and winners were $1000 First Prize - Karen Veverica, $300 Second Prize - Erica Newlands, and $200 Third Prize - Tammy Hammond. The famous Jamison Triplets were introduced (parents Robert & Louise Jamison). Entertainment was provided by Jim LaBanc, KT & Friends, Jason Kelly & Band, Roscoe Doubleday, Jr., Carolina Thumb Picker, and the Elgin Community Choir directed by Brian Heyward.

The 5:00 PM Closing Ceremonies "Under the Big Tent" and featured the Lugoff-Elgin ROTC unit with Johnny Potter as Master of Ceremonies with the Invocation given by Rev. Ken Jackson. Following the Pledge of Allegiance to the flag, the National Anthem was sung by Charles Becknell. Mayor James and Shari Few made a few remarks. The Blaney School Alma Mater was performed by author Doris Mattox and her daughters. The miniature Blaney Fire Truck raffle winner was announced and the Car Show trophies were awarded to "People's Choice" - Joe Langley, "Best Engine" - Robert Jones, and "Best of Show" - Ben Porter. Shirley Miles, Chairperson of the Centennial Committee, made closing remarks. After the singing of "America the Beautiful", a release of 100 balloons sent the crowd home happy.

An added attraction to the centennial festivities came on December 13, 2009, when the four-sided Seth Thomas Town Clock and 350 engraved bricks at Monument Square were dedicated in a ceremony at Town Hall. The rainy, cool day did not dampen the crowd's spirits as Senator Joel Lourie, Councilman C. R. Miles, Mayor Francis "Pete" James, and Chairperson Shirley Miles made appropriate remarks.

The mural, depicting the stages of Blaney-Elgin's development, painted on the side of the oldest building in town was created in March 2008 by Colt and Brent Shirley. The 1928 Warren Sanders store was the perfect place for the mural which depicts a train, the train depot, town clock, mules and wagon, and cotton fields.

Three new town welcome signs were erected in three town limits locations in Elgin showing the date the town was founded and "Home of the Catfish Stomp". The town will be forever grateful to Cliff Anderson of the Kershaw County Clean Community Committee for the $8000 grant used for the town signs and clock.

Town Council named the area around the new Town Clock, "Centennial Park" on February 2, 2010. On March 1, 2011, the Kershaw County Chamber of Commerce presented the town the Community Pride Award for their efforts in celebrating their 2008 Centennial and called attention especially to the new town clock and mural.

In 2012 the Centennial Committee evolved into the Blaney-Elgin Museum and Historical Society with 28 founding members. New members have joined in 2013 bringing the membership to 33.

The first Board of Directors elected were Shirley Miles, President; Anna Chason, Vice President; Donnelle Stockman, Secretary; Kenny Miles, Treasurer; and Doris Kling, Fred Davidson, and Johnny Potter, Board Members. The mission of this society is to protect, nurture, and support the historical, pre-historical, and cultural heritage of Blaney-Elgin through preservation, advocacy, and education.

The current major project for the Museum and Historical Society is to renovate a used building or build a museum to house artifacts now being donated to the Society. Fund raising for this project is essential to its completion and is an on-going challenge. Engraved bricks will still be sold to be installed in Centennial Park until the 3200 capacity is reached.

Seth Thomas Town Clock
Centennial Park
Elgin, S.C.

Salute to the Future…

Saturday, March 15, 2008, started out like any other day except the annual St. Patrick's Day Celebration in Columbia's Five Points was the destination of choice for many Elginites that day. But the air was noticeably still and heavy though there was not a cloud in the sky. It was not long before television and radio tornado warnings were being broadcast on every station in the Midlands. Then a tornado was spotted on the ground in Prosperity, and the National Weather Service warnings predicted tornados would move east across the Midlands. In Elgin, the weather increasingly worsened as rain became a sideways downpour due to the sharp increase in winds. Large hail began falling and visibility was zero. Objects were flying through the air as the destructive forces battered every barrier they came across. Then as suddenly as it began, it stopped, and the sun came out. An EF2 tornado had ripped right through the middle of downtown Elgin. A warehouse next to the Alton Nelson house was gone completely leaving only the concrete foundation. The Elgin House of Pizza had no roof; it lay on top of a nearby truck. Subdivisions near Bowen Street and Sessions Road were the pathway for the tornado's fury, damaging many homes.

Pine tree forests were bent almost completely over, all in the same direction. Many pine trees were snapped off completely and debris was everywhere. Good Aim Missionary Church near Tookiedoo was badly damaged looking more like a salvage yard than a house of worship. Sandhill Heights Baptist Church, west of Elgin and south of Tookiedoo, sustained significant shingle and siding damage with the front porch and steeple torn from the church.

In Prosperity, the EF3 tornado took two lives and caused tremendous damage to property. Amazingly, in Elgin, no lives were lost, and the citizens, true to form, rushed to aid their neighbors. Today all the damage has long since been repaired or replaced, and newly constructed homes are now safer one story and brick structures. There are more fields where trees used to be, and Good Aim Missionary Church has a new larger brick church building and a thriving congregation. Yes, Elgin has survived yet another storm of the many in its past because Blaney-Elgin is a place where there are people who care about one another. Blaney-Elgin's journey through the decades of the past has breathed new life into a future bright with promise.

Carpe diem.

CHURCH HISTORIES

1810	Smyrna United Methodist Church
1839	Harmony Baptist Church
1861	Union Baptist Church
1863	Green Hill Baptist Church
1870	Fort Clark Baptist Church
1905	Blaney Baptist Church
1914	Good Aim Missionary Baptist Church
1915	Highway Pentecostal Holiness Church
1936	High Hill Baptist Church
1942	Salem United Methodist Church
1956	Hillcrest Baptist Church
1972	Sandhill Heights Baptist Church

SMYRNA UNITED METHODIST CHURCH

On Twenty-Five Mile Creek on November 20, 1810, Methodists purchased 8 acres of land from Nathan Melton for $10, on which the following year they built a sanctuary that is still part of Smyrna United Methodist Church. At first, there were no church buildings, and the men constructed a tent made of tree branches for shade during meetings conducted by a circuit rider. Smyrna was founded by members who had been worshipping at a nondenominational Fairfield District Church called the Wolf Pit, where James Jenkins, a Methodist minister, was then preaching. Following a camp meeting at Sanders Creek, across the river in the Kershaw District, 80 members, including the Motley family, were converted to the Methodist Episcopal Church and withdrew and organized their own church.

John Motley was sent to America by the King of England before the Revolutionary War. After the war he remained in South Carolina and married Philippina Little and had several children. They lived in the Smyrna community between Camden and Winnsboro. John Motley and his children now lie in the Smyrna graveyard. His great grand-daughter, Mrs. Corrie Baucom, was active in the church until 2009 when God called her home.

Smyrna Church was built mostly by slaves using foot-wide green boards and was completed in 1811. Those same green boards set in place by slaves support the church building today. Rev. James Jenkins was listed on the church land deed as a member of the Board of Trustees, and before he moved on he led the church to complete the building.

Prior to the Civil War a local racing club used the church as a clubhouse, and the church received revenue from the races. During the Civil War the racetrack and church grounds were used for drilling and parade grounds by local Confederate troops. In 1865, marauding Union armies destroyed parts of the church building.

The people of Smyrna have a great heritage and by God's grace will continue the work begun under tents and in fields for hundreds of years to come.

HARMONY BAPTIST CHURCH

As far as can be determined from incomplete records, in 1771 or 1772 Twenty-Five Mile Creek Baptist Church was started as a branch of Congaree Baptist Church in the Richland District. It was founded by ministers Phillip Mulkey, Joseph Reese, Timothy Dargan, and Thomas Norris. It is not recorded which minister served as the first pastor. Around 1785 another branch was started at what is now Blythewood called Sandy Level Baptist Church. Sometime after that another branch called Bear Creek Baptist Church was founded in the Kershaw District. In the 1830s this church was moved about four miles east and its name changed to Harmony Baptist Church. The name Harmony first appeared in the minutes of the Bethel Association in 1839.

Harmony's first resident pastor, John T. Ross, served from 1858 until 1862.

The old white frame church building was moved to the present site on Tookiedoo Lane on logs used to roll it as it was pulled by mules. Over the years the log building was enlarged with the addition of classrooms and a kitchen. It was bricked and converted into Sunday School and fellowship space with the addition of the new sanctuary in the 1980s. The church converted the fellowship space in the original sanctuary to classrooms in 2003 after the completion of a new fellowship hall.

Harmony was involved with other churches from the beginning to minister to their community and to preach the Gospel. In 1863 Harmony withdrew from the Bethel Association to be one of the founding churches of the Fairfield Baptist Association that later became the Columbia Metro Baptist Association.

Some Harmony members from the Sand Hills area of the Kershaw District organized Union Baptist Church in 1861 due to the traveling distance and the deep sand roads which made it difficult for them to attend Harmony regularly. Both Harmony and Union Churches suffered damage as they were looted and pillaged by the Union troops of General Sherman who invaded Kershaw County in 1865.

Among the pastors serving in the 20th Century was Rev. A. L. Willis who was pastor during the great depression and the beginning of World War II. During his ministry the church added Sunday School rooms and electric lights. Other pastors included Rev. LaVon Cockrell who saw Sunday school attendance nearly double and guided the beginning of programs like the Women's Missionary Union, Training Union, and a Church Music program. The Church Music ministry became an important part of the church, and Harmony is known to have an excellent music program. Mr. Donnie Jacobs served for 30 years in the church music ministry and Mrs. Polly Crawley currently leads the music.

Rev. Paul K. Drum served the church during the 1950s and in 1960 Rev. K. W. Rabon became pastor. Through many pastorates Harmony has continued to grow in every facet. In 1963 Rev. H. T. McNeal became pastor and served for the next 25 years as pastor. Rev. McNeal was the first full time pastor. He built the first indoor baptistery, and the church membership nearly doubled during his ministry.

Rev. Bobby Lockwood served as pastor in the late 1980s until Rev. Jack Border became pastor. The church continued to grow during these years. In 1996, Rev. Chris Smith came as pastor. During his pastorate, Harmony continued to grow and built a fellowship building. Also during this time the church became more active in home and foreign missions. They took trips annually and helped found a church in Kentucky, they took their first international mission trip to Nicaragua, and became involved in Men's Ministry and Disaster Relief work with the South Carolina Baptist Convention.

In 2006, Dr. Dan Griffin came as pastor. The church has continued to be involved in Disaster Relief work doing chainsaw and debris removal as well as assessment work. They have added a garage to house the relief trailer and the bus used to pull the trailer. When the tornado hit Elgin in 2008, Dr. Griffin led the effort to clean up, and the Harmony chainsaw unit worked for two weeks doing volunteer work to help their neighbors. Harmony continues to work and partner with other churches in the Elgin Minister's Association, Kershaw and Columbia Associations, and with the community. The church has strengthened the Kentucky church, and members are involved in missions locally, nationally, and internationally.

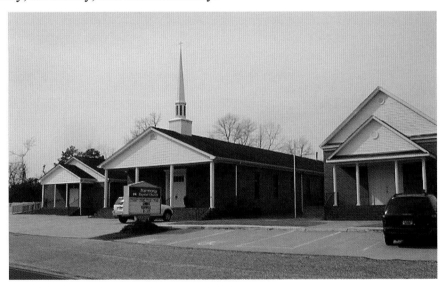

UNION BAPTIST CHURCH

The Union Baptist Church was first called Unionville, apparently from a nearby post office of that name, and was organized on October 6, 1861, with 29 members. Twenty-eight members had been regularly dismissed from the Harmony Baptist Church for the purpose of constituting a church near the Cureton Old Mill on Rice Creek Spring Road, Kershaw District, South Carolina.

The Charter members of the new church were John Bowen, Lewis Jinks, John Green, Muggy Evans, Thomas Jeffers, W. M. Sanders, Brown C. Ross, W. M. Ross, W. H. Sanders, Roderick McDonald, John Albert, Jessie McDonald, James Craft, Susan Albert, Harriet Green, Miriam Sanders, Louisa Evans, Tiny Jeffers, Matilda McDonald, Nancy Sanders, Susan Ross, Martha Ross, Elizabeth Manning, Catherine Ross, Elizabeth Ross, Anne Jinks, Harriet Motley, Nancy Long, and Mrs. Mary Ross from New Hope Church.

John Albert gave the land and a log house for the new church. The log house was used for the first church meeting house. The Rev. Brown C. Ross was called as their first Supply (Pastor). Rev. B. C. Ross served the church intermittently as pastor for 30 years. By 1863 there were 57 white members and 28 black members, a total of 85 members, and the church was a charter member of the Fairfield Baptist Association.

We must remember that the Unionville Church was organized only a few months after the beginning of the Civil War and that the early years were rife with the horrors of war making it difficult for the church to continue to exist, let alone prosper. The liberation of the slaves at the close of the Civil War reduced the membership from 85 to 55 or less. In 1881 the name Union appears in the minutes of the church instead of Unionville. Rev. Brown C. Ross is listed as pastor and Jesse T. Ross as clerk.

In 1899-1900, the Seaboard Railway was built with a station located about two miles from the Union Church. This brought a great change in the lives of the people living in the "Sand Hills" as well as an impact on the nearby slowly growing town of Blaney.

In 1892, the church reported 78 members with Rev. Brown C. Ross as pastor. In 1904, the Blaney Baptist Church was started which drew some of the members from Union, reducing its membership significantly.

The year 1910 brought an enlargement of the church grounds with two acres purchased for $12.50 per acre. The 32x60 sanctuary part of the present building was erected in 1911.

The aftermath of the "Great War" (WWI) of 1917 was marked by an inflation period followed by the Great Depression at the close of 1930. The serious financial condition of the nation mirrored the fiscal condition of the church, but the 260 members held on and kept the doors of the church open with great sacrifice. The Rev. A. L. Willis was the pastor at a salary of $240 a year.

A few times Union and Blaney used the same pastor: Rev. John Phillip Isenhower in 1908, Rev. J. B. Shivar in 1922, Rev. J. D. Harrelson in 1927, and Rev. W.S. Cromer in 1933. Each time the arrangements were made independently, and the pastors served part-time. The two churches' leadership discussed joining the two churches together but could never find agreement to accomplish the merger.

The Great Depression resulted in the closing of all banks in March 1933 by President Franklin D. Roosevelt. Contributions for church work were greatly reduced. The 250 members gave only $226.25 in all of 1932, and 1933 was worse.

Another adverse effect on the work of the church occurred in 1941 and throughout World War II, but a new day dawned with the calling of Rev. George R. Partridge who was the first full-time pastor in 1947. A home was constructed for the new pastor in 1947 at a cost of $3000.

Membership grew in 1947 to 205 with offerings of $1958, and in 1948 membership was 282 with offerings of $2025. The 1949 offerings grew to $3154 with 13 baptisms.

Mr. Sam Henry Ross was elected Deacon for Life on April 17, 1955, in honor of his active service as a deacon for 38 years, his faithfulness as a member, and his generous financial support of the church.

A reversal of fortunes occurred in 1956 as Pastor Rev. Richard Brookshire withdrew from the church, and sixty-six other Union members followed him because of doctrinal differences and formed Hillcrest Baptist Church in Blaney on Highway #1.

The Union Church weakened numerically and financially, again called Rev. George Partridge to be the pastor of the church. The former pastor accepted the call on July 15, 1956.

In 1958 the church building was brick veneered with other improvements and furnishings. The church had come a long way from the log cabin in 1861.

The Union Baptist Church has contributed to the formation of four other churches in the community: Blaney Baptist in 1905, Highway Pentecostal Holiness Church in 1915, Hillcrest Baptist Church in 1956, and Sandhill Heights Baptist Church in 1972.

The years rolled by, and many pastors and congregations toiled hard in the Lord's vineyard at Union Baptist Church, but the church wanted to do more in the community that had grown up around them. On January 20, 2008, Rev. Jerry Lewis and the congregation had a groundbreaking ceremony for a new gymnasium building to be constructed at the end of the existing fellowship hall. The 9600 sq. ft. gym would have a full size basketball court, volley ball set-up, restrooms, and equipment/seating storage. The gym was completed in October 2008 thanks to the vision and support of G. P. and Virginia Monroe as well as the entire Union congregation. Today the church is still in the same location it was in 1861, except the area is no longer known as Unionville and the road is no longer called Rice Creek Springs Road near the Cureton Old Mill. Today the church is on Wildwood Lane between Chestnut and Smyrna Roads, 2 miles north of Elgin, S. C.

Union Church congregation 1947 - 1950

GREEN HILL BAPTIST CHURCH

The Green Hill Baptist Church was founded in 1862 by Reverend Isom Outen. The first church was built in 1901. This building was erected on a hill in a brush arbor. The second church was built in 1905. The oral history passed down through the generations stated that the church edifice was equipped with a bell tower. The church had one choir (the senior choir) and four ushers.

In 1945, Green Hill Church was the only predominately African American church in the Lugoff-Elgin, S. C. sand hills community with a substantial congregation. In that same year some members left Green Hill to form High Hill Baptist Church.

A third edifice was erected in 1967, under the leadership of Reverend James Wilson. Services were held at this location on the second and fourth Sundays of each month. Deacon Robert Qualls was Chairman of the Board of Deacons. In 1981 Reverend Willie Tucker assumed the pastorate and a dining area was added to the church. Rev. Tucker served as pastor from 1981 to 1984. Deacon Johnny Gibbs was elected chairman of the board of deacons after Deacon Robert Qualls departed this life to be with our Lord.

In 1984 Reverend S. M. Hightower assumed the pastorate of the church. Under his leadership the vestibule sanctuary was remodeled and weekly services began. Deacon Calvin A. O'Neal was appointed as assistant chairman of the board of deacons. Rev. Hightower served through 1985.

In 1986, Reverend Dr. Billy J. Carter, Sr. was elected pastor. Under his leadership twelve have accepted their call to the gospel ministry. Four have been ordained as deacons. A modern palatial church edifice dedicated to our LORD Jesus Christ was erected. Dr. Carter is a first-class leader and progressive pastor/teacher who continued the legacy of ministerial excellence at Green Hill Baptist Church.

In 1993, the church began to distribute USDA foods to the community quarterly. In 2004, construction of our beautiful new sanctuary began led by Pastor Carter. The Building Committee consisted of Chairperson-Deacon Minnie Anthony, Evelyn Ware, Carolyn Benson and Robert Hudson. Subcommittee members were Rev. Alonzo Tucker, Deacon Freddie Williamson, Loretta Qualls, Barbara Gibbs, Rev. Melandie Portee, Lottie Lyles and Mary Hudson. The first service was held on Sunday, November 28, 2004, the 142nd anniversary of the church. The church was dedicated on Sunday, February 20, 2005 with the Reverend Walter Carter of Long Beach, California preaching the dedicatory message. Reverend Calvin A. O'Neal is presently serving as Interim Pastor.

We praise God for our ancestors who laid the spiritual and physical foundation of this church. Green Hill Baptist Church has over one-hundred and fifty years of proud Christian service to our community and the best is yet to come.

FORT CLARK BAPTIST CHURCH

Fort Clark was an outgrowth of Bethlehem Baptist Church, the first African American Baptist Church in West Wateree, Kershaw District. Pastor Anthony C. Jumper and the church leadership issued letters of dismissal to members living further away from Bethlehem who desired to form a new church for travel convenience.

On October 10, 1870, Fort Clark Baptist Church was organized with founding membership of approximately 55 under the leadership of an organizational council, Pastor Jumper, and Rev. Monroe Boykin. Services were first held under a brush arbor on land owned by Mr. Earl Talmadge Bowen.

In the late 1870s, an acre of land was purchased from Mr. E. T. Bowen on Veterans Row and Smyrna Rd., and a wooden structure was built. Lanterns were used for lighting and a pot-bellied stove for heat. Baptisms were conducted in a man-made pool using water from a near-by spring. This church building burned in the 1950s, the fire believed related to the activities of a local hate group. Mt. Sinai AME Church allowed Fort Clark members to worship in their church until a new brick facility was completed in 1957.

An education wing was added to this church building in the 1980s and additional land was purchased for future church growth. The 1990s saw renovations to the church, and in 1994 the sanctuary was expanded to seat about 300 people. In March 2000, the foundation was poured for the fellowship hall as the church continued to grow.

Nine pastors have led the church since its beginning:
Rev. Anthony Jumper 1870 - 1895.
Rev. Sandy A. Boyd (short lived ministry ending before 1920s)
Rev. Gist Murphy (believed to have served longer than any other)
Rev. Clarence Harrell
Rev. C. J. Britt
Rev. John C. Williams
Rev. Levi Bellamy
Rev. Tommy Rush 1982
Rev. William H. Woodard 1989 - Present

BLANEY BAPTIST CHURCH

Missionary Rev. H. R. Ezell was commissioned by the Executive Board of the Fairfield Baptist Association in 1903 to establish a church at Blaney, a new community in southwest Kershaw County on the Seaboard Railroad. Mr. Jesse T. Ross gave two acres of land for the church building. By the end of 1903 the church only had a roof and weatherboard up, yet the members in 1904 occupied the unfinished building under the leadership of Missionary Rev. John Phillip Isenhower.

It was March 12, 1905, before the members were officially organized into a Southern Baptist Church. A Sunday School of 60 pupils was begun, and an offering of $5.65 was received. The Rev. John Phillip Isenhower became the pastor with a salary of $100 per year. C. P. Ray was elected as the first church clerk. Ten new members were added to the church that day including Jesse T. Ross who moved his membership from Union Baptist Church in order to help the new church get a good start. He became church clerk and treasurer on December 14, 1905. Also on the same date the church voted to finish the church building. A collection of $6.19 was taken.

The church building was completed in 1908 which also was the year that the community of Blaney was incorporated into a town, January 23, 1908. The Rev. John Phillip Isenhower was elected as the first Intendent (Mayor) of the town of Blaney. Rev. Isenhower was Pastor of Blaney Baptist and Union Baptist Church during 1908 serving each on a part-time basis.

In 1909, Walter P. Miles was elected church clerk and W. H. Whaley was called as pastor at a salary of $200 per year. Boykin K. Rose became church clerk in 1922 and served 28 years, until 1950.

In the mid-1920s Blaney and Harmony built a parsonage which they jointly owned. In 1935 Blaney bought out Harmony's interest and became sole owner of the parsonage.

By 1945, the church building was in a "dilapidated" condition-- leaking, its pot-bellied stoves about worn out -- so the church voted to build a new church, not knowing how they would finance such a plan. The new church was built on a "hope and a prayer". New pews were bought in 1948 and in 1952 a new parsonage for $8562.71.

A new nine-room Sunday School wing was added to the church building in 1957 at a cost of $8000. and an organ purchased in 1962. Renovations of the sanctuary occurred in 1969 with stained glass windows, carpet, and a new piano. The first lifetime deacons, J. D. Watson, Sr. and Boykin K. Rose, were elected. A paid music director was called. In 1972 the Virginia McKittrick wing was added to the Sunday School space. The size of the auditorium was increased, and a vestibule was added, all for $40,000.

Over most of the church's history, a steady but slow growth was experienced, but the period from 1972-2008 was one of tremendous growth.
> In 1976 - the Boykin K. Rose Library was established.
> In 1977- a church secretary was hired.
> In 1978 - the Family Life Center was built for $150,000.
> In 1980 - the parsonage was sold & moved, pastor housing allowance began.
> In 1981 - a paved parking lot in old parsonage space.
> In 1986 - New church built and Daycare opened.

Greatest accomplishment of the church is hundreds of lives touched and reborn into the Kingdom of God. The venture of faith began in 1903 continues today and into tomorrow to the Glory of God.

<u>Pastors of Blaney Baptist Church</u>

1903	H. R. Ezell, Missionary	1938	B. F. Carson
1904	John Phillip Isenhower, Missionary	1943	R. G. Johnson
1905	John Phillip Isenhower, Pastor	1944	Matthew Rabon
1906	H. R. Chapman	1946	George Walker
1906	John Phillip Isenhower	1949	Monroe Smith
1916	W. H. Whaley	1953	B. C. Franklin
1919	L. H. Carter	1956	Dean Clyde
1922	J. B. Shiver	1970	William R. Yown
1927	J. D. Harrelson	1974	James W. Salter
1928	M. C. Padgett	1980	William Coates, Jr.
1931	A. L. Willis	1987	Frank Barnes
1933	Willie S. Cromer	1990	Lawrence Dennis
1936	Rev. Dabney	2006	Phillip Blankenship

GOOD AIM MISSIONARY BAPTIST CHURCH

The church was started in 1914 under a brush arbor about a mile or more north of the present location on Cherokee Blvd. in the Tookiedoo community near Elgin, S. C. The organizational group included Rev. A. D. Roberson, Deacon Charlie Bostic, Deacon Robert Whitaker, Deacon Frank Griffin, and Deacon Ramon Simons.

As the membership grew, Mr. Mattox donated an acre of land on which the church was built. In 1915 the church building was erected from unfinished pieces of plywood and other scrap pieces of building material giving an unfinished appearance. In 1959, the church was rebuilt. In 1975, the church was remodeled to include a kitchen, two bathrooms, a first aid room, and other new additions. In 1999, the church was again remodeled and purchased 0.3 acres of land adjacent to the church. In June 2003, the educational building was dedicated and named in honor of the late Rev. J. H. Roberson, Sr. In 2007, the church changed the name of the church to include "Missionary".

On March 15, 2008, a tornado destroyed the 94-year-old church. Gravestones were uprooted and trees were blown down. The entire community came to help the church clean up the debris and salvage as much as possible of the destroyed church. On Sunday, March 16, 2008, the church service was held in the parking lot. The Easter service was held at Round Top Elementary School. The Bethel Baptist Church also gave the use of their old sanctuary for church services. The Mount Seirs Baptist Church opened their doors to Good Aim until the rebuilding of the church was complete.

Lyles and Lyles Construction Company began the rebuilding on September 14, 2009, and the groundbreaking ceremony was held on July 18, 2009. The church was completed on July 10, 2010.

Ministers who received their calling through or have roots in Good Aim are Rev. Benjamin Corley, Rev. Bruce W. Branch, Rev. Johnny Geiger, Rev. Clyburn Martin, Rev. A. D. Roberson, Rev. B. R. Roberson, Rev. J. C. Roberson, Rev. W. D. Roberson, Rev. Edwin Roberson, Elder Garfield Roberson, Rev. Evenly Ford, Rev. J. H. Roberson, Rev. Tommie Williams, Rev. Neil Simons, Rev. Travis Simons, and Rev. Willie Simons.

Pastors who have served Good Aim include:
Rev. Isaac Outten
Rev. Ferguson
Rev. Peay
Rev. Jackson
Rev. I. B. Butler
Rev. Gordon (served 24 years)
Rev. E. W. Hagan - 1959
Rev. J. H. Roberson, Sr. - 1961-1994
Rev. Michael D. Buckson - 1996-1998
Rev. Willie C. Simons - 1999-Present

Good Aim has been blessed with people who have been faithful in service over the years. The elderly members have modeled a steadfast faith, commitment, and love that continues to inspire everyone. As the church moves forward, God gives us the strength to meet the challenges of today giving us a powerful testimony about His redemptive grace. Our hearts are forever grateful for all that He has done; His church is complete and the blessings go on. Praise the Lord.

HIGHWAY PENTECOSTAL HOLINESS CHURCH

The Highway Church began in 1915 when land was donated by John Heath and lumber by Mr. Heath and Elmore Brown. The first structured church was built around 1921. As the Lord blessed, the church grew and they built a larger church in 1945 under the leadership of Rev. John W. Swails. Growth continued, and in 1958 a third church was constructed under the leadership of Rev. Marvin Cannon. The church built its first fellowship building in 1964 under the direction of Rev. N. D. Sellers.

The present parsonage and fellowship building began under the leadership of Rev. Mendel Stalvey, who pastored from 1970 to 1977. In 1978, the buildings were completed during the pastorate of Rev. Ned Owens. God continued to bestow His blessings on the church.

Rev. Jimmy Floyd came to pastor in 1984. Under his leadership renovation began in the sanctuary. During the period of construction, services were held in the fellowship building. The mortgage was burned in 1992.

Rev. George Cashwell became pastor in July 1995. The church voted to complete the upstairs of the educational building, adding another bathroom and additional classrooms and storage in 1996.

Roll Call of Pastors... (HIGHWAY PENTICOSTAL HOLINESS CHURCH)

1917	Rev. J. M. Legrande	1942	Rev. Rufus Bigby
1918-1919	Rev. R. J. Hodge	1943	Rev. George Pierce
1920	Rev. W. L. Brown	1944-1946	Rev. John Swails
1921	Rev. C. H. Culclasure	1947	Rev. C. T. Powell
1922-1923	Rev. R. J. Hodge	1948	Rev. W. T. Jeffers
1924	Rev. D. D. Causey	1949-1951	Rev. Leo Edwards
1925	Rev. Mack Chambers	1952-1954	Rev. Leonard Gardner
1926-1927	Rev. J. E. Bouknight	1955-1957	Rev. Wylie Evans
1928	Rev. H. K. Lemmons	1958-1962	Rev. M. O. Cannon
1929-1930	Rev. A. M. Graves	1962-1970	Rev. N. D. Sellers
1931	Rev. F. M. Britton	1970-1978	Rev. Mendel Stalvey
1932-1934	Rev. C. H. Culclasure	1978-1982	Rev. Ned Owens
1935	Rev. H. J. Gladden	1982-1984	Rev. Wylie Evans
1936-1938	Rev. J. M. Goude	1984-1995	Rev. Jimmy O. Floyd
1939	Rev. L. M. Goude	1996-2004	Rev. George Cashwell
1940-1941	Rev. R. L. Levine	2004-Present	Rev. Paul Miles

Visitation-Rev. Jim Rogers
Youth-Rev. Tim Sessions and
Rev. Brandon Goff

Highway Pentecostal Holiness Church's greatest years are her tomorrows.

HIGH HILL BAPTIST CHURCH

The building of High Hill Baptist Church was completed in 1936 after being under construction for an undetermined period of time. The location is 849 Watts Hill Road in the Elgin, S. C. area with a Lugoff address for mail.

The first Pastor was Rev. Emmanuel M. Jones.
The current Pastor is the Rev. David Stratford III.

The Missions Statement for the church…
"A community of belevers, motivated by the love of Jesus Christ, committed to fulfill the Great Commission through worship, proclaiming, ministry, discipleship, family fellowship, and mission."
Matthew 28:19-20

SALEM UNITED METHODIST CHURCH

The first service was held in the present Salem United Methodist Church in January 1942. After the old Salem Church closed in 1939, due to the World War II expansion of the Fort Jackson reservation, services were held in the Blaney School Auditorium. E. T. Bowen and Jesse T. Ross, Sr. donated land in the town of Blaney for a new church. Dewey Brazell and Fred Miles did the construction. The new church was a blending of members from Salem M. E. Church South at Fort Jackson, St. Paul Methodist Church on Old Wire Road, and new families in the Blaney community.

Later additions to the church included the vestibule, steeple, side wings for classrooms, kitchen, social hall, and the altar area. The first piano was donated by Dr. William Duncan Grigsby, the community physician. A major renovation funded by the Bowen family extended the length of the church and added an open altar area with a stained glass window depicting Christ at prayer in Gethsemane. The current parsonage was completed in 1961 on Surrey Lane. During the 1970s the original windows were replaced with stained glass windows depicting events in the life of Christ. A separate social hall was built in 1983 through the generosity of the Bowen family. The historical monument was added in 2012. The church today is the result of numerous gifts and countless hours of work and love by numerous donors.

From origins dating back to 1887, when the Salem M.C. Church South was located in Richland County (now Fort Jackson property), the church has celebrated seventy plus years in the present location. John Wesley, founder of Methodism, came to Charleston, South Carolina, in 1737 and began the work that has lasted 276 years.

HILLCREST BAPTIST CHURCH

On Sunday morning, February 19, 1956, sixty-six members of Union Baptist Church, including the pastor and his wife (Rev. and Mrs. Richard J. Brookshire), requested their letters in order to form a new church in the Blaney community. That afternoon, the group met at the present church site south of the Blaney town limits on U. S. IIighway #1, on land given by Mr. and Mrs. Ira O. Goff, to break ground for the church auditorium. The next day construction began under the supervision of Mr. Cranshaw Branham.

On April 1, 1956, while the auditorium was still under construction, the first service, an Easter Morning Sunrise Service, was conducted. The first regular worship service was conducted on May 27, 1956, in the completed auditorium. The church was constituted into the Hillcrest Baptist Church on July 22, 1956 with eighty-three charter members. The church set the Sunday nearest July 22 as the date for annual Homecoming Day Services each year.

2/19/1956	Rev. R. J. Brookshire
	Led to form new church, constructed auditorium, first floor of educational bldg. Purchased cemetery land.
7/7/1959	Rev. Furman Harvey
	Built pastorium and added second floor to Educ. Bldg.
6/20/1965	Rev. Ned Calvert
	Started Unified Budget System & bricked church.
6/17/1967	Rev. Charles W. Kirby
	Church renovations began & organ installed.
9/1/1971	Rev. Furman Harvey
	Fellowship Bldg. built, mortgage paid off, church steeple & improvements on church property.
2/22/1981	Rev. Tommy Huddleston
	Renovated auditorium & old educational bldg. , 2-story educational bldg. constructed and debt paid.
	Church gave birth to Pontiac First Baptist Mission.
2/17/1985	Rev. Furman Harvey designated "Pastor Emeritus".
6/19/1988	Rev. Bill Drees
	Purchased 5 acres land for mission church.
	Renovation and expansion of Fellowship Hall.
	Pontiac First Baptist constituted as church 7/14/1991.
	In 1995, Vision 2000, a 5-year growth plan adopted.
11/1/2001	Pastorate of Rev. Kenneth Jackson who has assisted and overseen the church in the following ministry endeavors:

The hiring of a full-time Minister of Children and Youth.
Began the Awana Children's Bible Ministry.
Mission work overseas in Romania, Peru, and Russia.
Mission work in New York and Pittsburgh.
Local mission outreach projects such as "Sacks of Love"
  food ministry at local elementary school serving over
  40 children annually.
Active Senior Adult Ministry as well as children's and
  youth activities.
Women's and Men's ministry groups.
Annual Ladies Brunches with guest speakers.

SANDHILL HEIGHTS BAPTIST CHURCH

Sandhill Heights had its beginning in October 1972 when twenty-six members of Union Baptist Church in Elgin decided to form a new church. Their first meeting place was in the chapel of the former Richland County Convalescent Home near Pontiac. As the membership grew, the members made plans to build a church sanctuary. Claude Motley secured a site on Bowen Street near Elgin, S. C., from McRae (Mac) Kirkland. George Watts, Claude Motley, Woodrow Ross, and Jack Flynn secured a former Army barracks from Fort Jackson and moved it to the new site. Church members and friends devoted countless hours renovating the barracks into a simple sanctuary, office, kitchenette, and three Sunday School rooms.

The first worship service was held May 6, 1973, in the newly renovated Sandhill Heights Baptist Church which is located at 2992 Bowen Street, west of Elgin, north of Pontiac and south of Tookiedoo. Rev. George R. Partridge, a retired pastor from Union Baptist Church, delivered the first sermon.

Charter members were Alton and Maude Nelson, Woodrow Ross, Thelma Ross Knapp, Thelma "Ted" Knapp Boykin, Claude and Belle Motley, Claude Motley Jr., Don and Jeanette Motley Fulmer, Robin Motley, Sylvia and Jack Flynn, Larry and Betty Flynn, Ronnie & Greg Flynn, Sam and Minnie Motley, Cathy and Lavon Watts, Mike Motley, Judge and Ida Lee Motley, Teri Motley, Frank and Ann Motley, George and Eva Watts, Curtis Pierce, Calvin and Maggie Joyner, and Donald Grigsby.

Rev. Fred Ayers, retired pastor of Dentsville Baptist Church, was called as the first pastor. Many dedicated servants of God have served in the pulpit including Rev. Furman Harvey, Rev. Eddie Short, Rev. Willie Cromer, Rev. Charles Miller, Rev. Carl Watts, Rev. Lonnie Watford, and Rev. Roger Snipes. Rev. Lanny Brisendine has served as pastor since 2010.

The church has undergone numerous additions, renovations, and modernizations since 1973. The original wooden structure has been bricked, a fellowship hall and larger kitchen was added, the sanctuary's low flat ceiling was converted to a vaulted ceiling, stained glass windows were added and dedicated in honor or memory of members, covered porches and handicapped ramps were added, and additional Sunday School rooms were added.

The church's exterior sustained significant damage from the Elgin tornado of March 2008. In addition to shingle and siding damage, the front porch and steeple were torn from the church. Repairs were rapidly made by church members.

Current weekly services include Sunday School, Sunday worship services, and Wednesday evening Bible study and prayer meeting. The Women's Missionary Union and Men's Brotherhood meet monthly and an active puppet ministry is ongoing. The church participates in the annual Elgin Catfish Stomp parade and the Lights of Lugoff Parade.

Sandhill Heights Baptist Church continues to serve as a place of worship for believers in the Elgin community.

MAYORS & INTENDENTS

TOWN OF BLANEY-ELGIN
1908-2013

1908	John Phillip Isenhower	Pastor @ Blaney & Union Baptist Churches
1909-1915	Jesse T. Ross	Postmaster/Merchant/Farmer
1916-1931	Unknown	
1932-1934	J. Paul Ross	Merchant
1935	Unknown	
1936-1937	John Henry Rabon, Sr.	Railroad Section Foreman @ Blaney
1938	Samuel W. Rose	Farmer
1939	J. Paul Ross	
1940-1946	Unknown	
1947-1948	Samuel W. Rose	
1949-1952	Unknown	
1953-1954	Robert A. Cochran	Blaney Physician
1955-1963	Ernest C. Potter, Jr.	Merchant
1964-1965	J. Don Watson, Jr.	Postmaster
1965-1971	Ernest C. Potter	
1971-1979	Charlie Wray Wooten	Businessman
1979-1983	James Suggs	Home Builder
1983-1987	Francis E. "Pete" James	Insurance/Magistrate
1987-1991	Loretta Ross Carr	Housewife
1991-1994	Francis E. "Pete" James	
1994-2007	Paul L. Grooms	Watch Plant/Meat Cutter
2007-2011	Francis E. "Pete" James	
2011	Brad Hanley	Accountant

Current Mayor, Brad Hanely
Photo by Judy Darby-Buchanan

TERMS

One Year	1908-1967
Two Years	1967-1974
Four Years	1974-Present

COUNCIL MEMBERS & WARDENS
TOWN OF BLANEY-ELGIN
1908-2013

1908	J.B. Cooper, B. B. Crisp, R.W.J. Kennedy, T.M. McCaskill
1913	W.F. Duke, J.G. Feaster, W.L. Miles, T.W. Watson
1933	J.P. Ross, W.D. Grigsby, J.G. Ross, E.T. Bowen
1938	J.P. Ross, W.D. Grigsby, J.G. Ross, E.T. Bowen
1954	E.T. Bowen, Ed Campbell, J.M. Wilson, J.T. Motley
1955	J.P. Ross, N.K. Rose, J.G. Ross, Ed Campbell
1957	Paul Ross, Jr.
1963	N.K. Rose, Dan Kelly, T.E. Campbell, C.R. Bowen
1964-65	Dan Kelly, Jack Ross, E.C. Potter, G.D. Goodwin
1966-67	Marvin Campbell, Dan Kelly, Jack Ross, G.D. Goodwin
1967	2-YEAR TERMS BEGIN
1970	J. T. Motley
1971	J.D. Watson, Sr., Jack Ross, J.T. Motley, Dan Kelly
1973	Eva Bowen, Wayne Sanders, Arthur Branham, W. D. McIntyre
1974	4-YEAR TERMS BEGIN- 2 year elections for rotation of council
1975-76	Eva Bowen, Paul Grooms, Francis E. James, A.B. Branham
1979	Francis E. James, Arthur Branham, Larry Owens, J.T. Motley
1981	Loretta Carr, Marshall Danenberg, Francis E. James, J.T. Motley
1983	Loretta Carr, Michael Gilchrist, Roger Ross, Bryce Smith
1985	Paul Grooms, Frank W. Thompson, Bryce Smith, Jim Wheaton
1987	Margie Howard, Bruce Sloan, Paul Grooms, Bryce Smith
1989	Roger Ross, J.F. Storemski, Paul Grooms, Bryce Smith
1991	Madge Strickland, Paul Grooms, Roger Ross, J.F. Storemski
1993	Madge Strickland, Paul Grooms, John Storemski, Joe Romer
1995	John Storemski, Joe Romer, Norman Ernst, Walter C. Coleman
1997	William Salter, John Storemski, Joe Romer, Norman Ernst
1998	D. Todd McDonald
1999	William Salter, John Storemski, Don Williams, Anthony Payne
2001	John Storemski, Anthony Payne, Freddie Grant, Freddie Heath
2003	Bill Salter, Don Williams, Anthony Payne, John Storemski
2005	Melissa Emmons, John Storemski, Scott Jacobs, Brad Hanley
2007	Brad Hanley, Jerry Jeffers, Scott Jacobs, John Storemski
2009	Larry Risvold, Roger Ross, Brad Hanley, John Storemski
2011	Norman Ernst, Melissa Emmons, Roger Ross, Larry Risvold
2013	Edward Smith, Dana Sloan, Melissa Emmons, Candace Silvers

BLANEY-ELGIN TOWN CLERKS
1933-2013

1933	Bonnie Cooper
1938	Mary Rabon
1948	Mattie Ross
1954	Clara E. Goodwin
1955	Gladys Potter
1962	Thelma Kelly
1963	Betty D. Brown
1964	Thelma Kelly
1965	Mary R. Hudson
1967	Thelma Kelly
1971	Leila Ross
1973	Julia S. Bobo
1975	Eva Garnes
1975	Camille Burney
1975	George M. Maxwell
1977	Harriet G. Jeffers
1981	Nettie Campbell
1995	Judy Darby-Buchannan
2013	Beth Hyman

CHIEF MUNICIPAL JUDGES
1977-2013

1977	Jim Suggs
1979	Phillip Pia
1983	Barbara Codere
1985	Edgar M. March
1987-2010	W.R. "Bill" Hyman
1997	Clarence Chavis, Associate
2010	David Reuwer
2011	Dennis Arledge, Associate

FIRE & POLICE DEPARTMENTS
TOWN OF BLANEY-ELGIN
1940-2013

FIRE CHIEF			POLICE CHIEF	
1964	E. C. Potter, Jr.		1940	Stanley Rose
1968	J. Don Watson, Jr.		1940-48	A. J. Huckabee
1970	Ray Strickland		1944-45	H. W. Sanders
1971	Donald D. Carr		1948	Fred Hunter
1973	Wayne Sanders		1965	Harold McCoy
1973	Charlie Emanuel		1971	Donald D. Carr
1973	Curtis Pierce		1973	Curtis Pierce
1979	Paul Grooms		1975	W. R. Sturkie
1984	John Potter		1976	G. H. Gerald
1989	Allen Robinson		1979	Clarence Chavis
1991	David Bagwell		1981	Luther G. Dyson
1994	Thomas Jaye Buff		1989	Dennis McKelvey
1995	George Marthers		1992	Kelly Johnson
1997	Terri Kearns		1993	Ernie DeBruhl
1998-99	George Marthers		1993	Harold Brown
2000	Lewis Booth			
2003	Tammy Branham			
2004	George Marthers			

Appendix 5   Blaney-Elgin Voting Precincts/Changes

Year		Voting Place	Poll Managers
1824		Cureton's Mill	E. Cureton, A. Watkins, John Whitaker
1828		Cureton's Mill	John Motley, Wm. Rabb, George Willie
1829		Cureton's Mill	D. Montgomery, John Motley, Wm. Rabb
1830		Cureton's Mill	Unknown
1832		Cureton's Mill	Unknown
1845		Cureton's Mill	F. Bowen, D. Motley, John Motley
1851		Cureton's Mill	F. Bowen, John Motley, JP Richbourg
1859		Cureton's Mill	F. Bowen, JJ Huckabee, Adam Team
1864		Cureton's Mill	F. Bowen, Emanuel Parker, James Team
1872		Cureton's Mill	E. Parker (DEM) (Party appt.-US Court)
1876		Cureton's Mill	Voting and Tax Collection Site
1900		Cureton's Mill	CA Bowen, JT Ross, JM Thornton
		(Traditional Voting Place for more than 75 years)	
1907		Blaney	RWJ Kennedy, JD Faust, JW Bradley
1914	(1)	Blaney PO	GE Hinson, JT Ross, SE Ross
	(2)	Harmony Ch.	TM Mattox, TM McCaskill
1916		Blaney	JW Bradley, JD McLendon, WH Simpson
			JS Ross, LB Sessions, WH Wood
1920	(1)	Blaney	US 19th Amendment - Women's Vote
	(2)	Harmony	
1964			US Civil Rights Act -
1974			Blaney Election Commission Estb.
			Ray Strickland, Eva Garnes, Pete James

County Dir. Voter Registration & Elections - Rosalind Watson
County Elections Board Commissioner - Judy Brock

Year		Voting Place	Poll Managers
2004	(1)	Blaney Bap. Ch.	George & Iris Conoly
	(2)	Blaney Elem Sch.	
2008	(1)	Blaney Bap. Ch.	George Conoly, Clk.
	(2)	Blaney Elem.Sch.	Pat Gormon, Clk.
	(3)	Elgin Town Hall	Madge Strickland, Clk.
	(4)	Harmony Bap. Ch.	
	(5)	Stover Middle Sch.	
2012	(6)	Blaney Fire Sta.	Damon Washington, Clk.

<u>**ELGIN COMMUNITY**</u>

<u>**OUTSTANDING CITIZENS OF THE YEAR**</u>
<u>**1977-2012**</u>

1977-78	**REV. JIM SALTER**
1979-80	**CHARLIE WRAY WOOTEN**
1983	**MARGIE HOWARD**
1985	**REV. BILL COATES**
1986	**FRANCIS E. "PETE" JAMES**
1987	**J. DON WATSON, JR.**
1990	**C. RAY MILES**
1991	**GEORGE MARTHERS**
1992	**CARL & MARY BROWN**
1993	**DAVID BAGWELL**
1994	**NETTIE MOAK CAMPBELL**
1995	**CHIEF HAROLD BROWN**
1996	**JUDGE W. R. "BILL" HYMAN**
1997	**THURSTON E. GOFF**
1998	**PAUL L. GROOMS**
2000	**PRESTON H. GOFF**
2001	**VICTOR MARTHERS**
2002	**KATHY MOAK BROWN**
2003	**A. T. "HAMMY" MOAK**
2004	**MELISSA EMMONS**
2005	**REV. KEN JACKSON**
2006	**TONY BONDS**
2007	**MAXINE CAMPBELL**
2008	**GLENNA BROWN KAISER**
2009	**BILL TAFEL**
2010	**LARRY & SOFIE COLLINS**
2011	**SHIRLEY S. MILES**
2012	**DORIS K. KLING**

BIBLIOGRAPHY

Libraries, Archives, and Museums

Elgin Museum and Historical Society, Elgin, SC
Town of Elgin Minutes and Records 1908-2013, Elgin, SC
Elgin Branch Library, Elgin, SC
Camden Archives and Museum, Camden, SC

Newspapers

Camden Chronicle, Camden, S. C. (Archived)
Camden Confederate 1861
Camden Journal 1872
Chronicle-Independent, Camden, S. C. (Archived)
Columbia Record 1912
Kershaw Gazette 1872, 1876
The Elgin News, Elgin, S. C. 2008-2013
The May Times, DuPont Plant, Camden, S. C. (Selected)
The State, Columbia, S. C. (Selected)

Published Sources, Books and Articles

Guide to Selected Historical Sites in Kershaw County/District
(Pub by Kershaw County Historical Society, Camden, 1992)
Kershaw County Legacy - A Commemorative History
(Pub Kershaw County Bicentennial Commission, Camden, 1976)
Kershaw County 1850 Census Expanded Genealogical Information
(Pub Camden, 1977, Catawba-Wateree Genealogical Society)
Kirkland & Kennedy. *Historic Camden: Colonial and Revolutionary,* Columbia, S. C.
1905
SC Postcards, Col. VII, Kershaw County, Charleston, 2002
(Howard Woody & Davie Beard)
A History of Kershaw County, S. C., Columbia, USC Press 2011
(Joan A. Inabinet and L. Glen Inabinet)
Centennial History of Union Baptist Church, Blaney, S. C.
 A Century Story of Trial and Triumph 1861-1961
(William C. Allen, Pub Vogue Press, Columbia, S. C. 1961)

Index

AUTHOR'S POSTLUDE

My hope is that you who read this historical account will appreciate as never before our Sand Hills ancestors whose resourcefulness matched their courage in their search for a better life. Our earliest generations exhibited rugged determination as they wove together a beautiful tapestry of hope, honest toil, bravery, and fortitude. The generations since have added distinct strands of community cooperative effort to enlarge and enrich our honored traditions. It is our challenge, not only to preserve this tapestry for future generations, but to sculpt our own inspirational living legacy lessons into this historical life-line.

Madge Black Strickland

"Whatever you do...Work at it with all your heart, as working for the Lord."   **Colossians 3:23**

Madge is married to Ray Carl Strickland of Elgin, S.C., and is the mother of five sons, Terry, Larry, Tony, David and Daniel. She enjoys eleven grandchildren and seven great-grandchildren. She graduated from Blaney High School in 1950 and retired as an Administrative Officer from the United States Department of Agriculture in 1989 with 35 years service. She briefly entered local politics, serving on the Elgin Town Council 1991-1994 and on the Lugoff-Elgin Water Board 1994-1995. She retired again in 2009 from Baptist Church Music Director Ministries spanning 45 years. She is the author of "Believe in the Grass", a memoir (2009), "RISE", an inspirational hand-me-down cookbook (2010), and "Madgic Measures", a gardening guide (2011).